1,000,000 Books

are available to read at

Forgotten Books

www.ForgottenBooks.com

Read online
Download PDF
Purchase in print

ISBN 978-1-332-30316-8
PIBN 10311479

This book is a reproduction of an important historical work. Forgotten Books uses state-of-the-art technology to digitally reconstruct the work, preserving the original format whilst repairing imperfections present in the aged copy. In rare cases, an imperfection in the original, such as a blemish or missing page, may be replicated in our edition. We do, however, repair the vast majority of imperfections successfully; any imperfections that remain are intentionally left to preserve the state of such historical works.

Forgotten Books is a registered trademark of FB &c Ltd.
Copyright © 2018 FB &c Ltd.
FB &c Ltd, Dalton House, 60 Windsor Avenue, London, SW19 2RR.
Company number 08720141. Registered in England and Wales.

For support please visit www.forgottenbooks.com

1 MONTH OF FREE READING

at
www.ForgottenBooks.com

By purchasing this book you are eligible for one month membership to ForgottenBooks.com, giving you unlimited access to our entire collection of over 1,000,000 titles via our web site and mobile apps.

To claim your free month visit:
www.forgottenbooks.com/free311479

* Offer is valid for 45 days from date of purchase. Terms and conditions apply.

English
Français
Deutsche
Italiano
Español
Português

www.forgottenbooks.com

Mythology Photography **Fiction** Fishing Christianity **Art** Cooking Essays Buddhism Freemasonry Medicine **Biology** Music **Ancient Egypt** Evolution Carpentry Physics Dance Geology **Mathematics** Fitness Shakespeare **Folklore** Yoga Marketing **Confidence** Immortality Biographies Poetry **Psychology** Witchcraft Electronics Chemistry History **Law** Accounting **Philosophy** Anthropology Alchemy Drama Quantum Mechanics Atheism Sexual Health **Ancient History Entrepreneurship** Languages Sport Paleontology Needlework Islam **Metaphysics** Investment Archaeology Parenting Statistics Criminology **Motivational**

LIBRARY
OF THE
UNIVERSITY OF CALIFORNIA.

Class

**COLLEGE
HISTORIES
OXFORD**

WORCESTER COLLEGE

" ... cit Dominus sic domui huic"

University of Oxford
COLLEGE HISTORIES

CESTER COLLEGE

BY

C. HENRY DANIEL, M.A.
FELLOW, BURSAR, AND SOMETIME TUTOR OF WORCESTER COLLEGE
FELLOW OF KING'S COLLEGE, LONDON

W. R. BARKER, B.A.
SOMETIME SCHOLAR OF WORCESTER COLLEGE

LONDON
F. E. ROBINSON & CO.
20 GREAT RUSSELL STREET, BLOOMSBURY
1900

University of Oxford

COLLEGE HISTORIES

BY

C. HENRY DANIEL, M.A.

FELLOW, BURSAR, AND SOMETIME TUTOR OF WORCESTER COLLEGE
FELLOW OF KING'S COLLEGE, LONDON

AND

W. R. BARKER, B.A.

SOMETIME SCHOLAR OF WORCESTER COLLEGE

LONDON
F. E. ROBINSON & CO.
20 GREAT RUSSELL STREET, BLOOMSBURY
1900

LF735
D2

NERAL

TO

WORCESTER COLLEGE

THE PROVOST, FELLOWS, SCHOLARS, AND

ALL OTHER MEMBERS OF THAT

SOCIETY

120061

PREFACE

THE divided authorship of this volume is the chief matter that requires explanation in the Preface. When I first began to work on the volume it was intended that I should devote especial attention to the monastic part, and to a further elucidation, if possible, of the Greek College scheme. The remaining chapters were to be in Mr. Daniel's hands, though I was to give him such additional information as I came across in the course of my reading, and Mr. Daniel was to take the general responsibility for the entire volume.

Unfortunately, when all the material for Mr. Daniel's portion of the work had already been completed, and the time was drawing very close when it would be necessary to send the volume to the printer, Mr. Daniel was disabled by an accident, which rendered it impossible for him to devote himself to the work for many weeks. In consequence of this I took over the material for the remaining chapters which had accumulated in Mr. Daniel's hands, and, as a matter of fact, finished the text of the book.

But though I am mainly responsible for certain chapters, I must acknowledge my indebtedness to

Mr. Daniel for the whole book. The short studies of College history which he has written in the past have in almost all cases suggested the directions in which to look for such additional facts as are embodied in this volume; and this volume only really fills in the outlines which he had already sketched out. He has also looked through the proofs of the entire volume, and made many valuable additions and corrections.

I must acknowledge myself specially indebted to Mr. T. W. Jackson for the great assistance he has rendered me in connection with the history of Gloucester College. Many years ago he made a study of this part of the College history, dealing with the matter in a far wider way than has been possible to me. He very kindly consented to look through these early chapters, both in manuscript and proof, and his invaluable suggestions have saved me from many serious errors. In addition to this, he has given me information which has cleared up several disputed points. In particular, the identification of the Pershore chamber, the information with regard to Bury St. Edmunds, and as to the Cambridge Benedictines, and part of the information as to the Abbey of Malmesbury, are due to him. Perhaps one may be allowed to express a hope that the fruit of his researches will some day be published.

I must also acknowledge my debt to the Provost, who very kindly gave me the fullest facilities for examining the College books and the portraits in the Provost's lodgings; to Mr. W. H. Hadow, who kindly furnished me with notes in reference to the field scheme; to Mr. Berington and Mr. A. R. Bayley, both of Malvern, the former for giving me permission to copy some manuscripts in his possession, and the latter for examining the manuscripts; to the Dean of Canterbury and the Librarian of the Dean and Chapter of Canterbury for procuring for me the copy of a deed in the Chapter Library; and to the officials of the Boat Club for granting me the loan over an extended period of their interesting minute book.

Lastly, as to the general scope of the book, we may say that the early periods of the College history have been treated rather more fully than the later periods, because they deal with a portion of the University system which has never been, as far as we know, very fully treated, and because in recent years the College has been fortunate in possessing no history.

W. R. BARKER.

CONTENTS

CHAPTER	PAGE
I. THE FOUNDATION OF GLOUCESTER COLLEGE	1
II. SOURCES OF HISTORY—NUMBERS IN GLOUCESTER COLLEGE—THE MONASTERIES AND THE COLLEGE—CAMERÆ AND ANCIENT BUILDINGS	14
III. THE RELATIONS OF ST. ALBANS AND GLOUCESTER COLLEGE	40
IV. THE COLLEGE SYSTEM—EXPENSES OF THE BENEDICTINE STUDENTS — THE LAST YEARS OF THE COLLEGE—DISTINGUISHED MEMBERS OF GLOUCESTER COLLEGE	57
V. THE DISSOLUTION — THE BISHOP OF OXFORD'S PALACE—THE FOUNDATION AND PROGRESS OF GLOUCESTER HALL	89
VI. DEGORY WHEARE — THE CIVIL WAR AND THE RESTORATION—BYROM EATON—THE MEMBERS OF GLOUCESTER HALL	105
VII. DR. WOODROFFE AND THE GREEK COLLEGE	128
VIII. THE FOUNDATION OF WORCESTER COLLEGE	154
IX. WORCESTER COLLEGE IN THE EIGHTEENTH AND NINETEENTH CENTURIES	182

CONTENTS

CHAPTER	PAGE
X. BENEFACTIONS	201
XI. CHAPEL—LIBRARY—HALL—THE GARDENS—PLATE—PICTURES—THE COLLEGE ARMS—REGISTERS—BIBLE-CLERKS—FELLOW-COMMONERS—THE RIVER—THE UNDERGRADUATE	213

APPENDICES

A. AUTHORITIES	247
B. THE NORTHERN CAMERÆ	255
C. THE MEMBERS OF GLOUCESTER HALL	256
D. THE PRESENT CONSTITUTION OF THE COLLEGE	258
INDEX	261

ST. ALBANS AND GLOUCESTER COLLEGE 43

all parts of the kingdom, they used to speak of his magnificence and his holiness, and to increase the number of his friends and to refute his enemies."

In addition to this he contributed more than £40 to the repair of the house and furniture of the scholars, he gave £20 to support his scholars, and he gave as much more in alms out of his private purse.

To John de la Moote belongs the credit of beginning the stone house for the scholars at Oxford. Owing to the fortunate accident of his short tenure of office, we are enabled to fix the date of the St. Albans buildings at Gloucester College to within five years. When he entered on his abbacy, he observed that the houses of his scholars at Oxford were of wood and very ancient, and in a ruinous condition. Moreover, they were unpleasant owing to their vicinity to the kitchen, and not large enough to hold all the scholars he had decided to send, so he began to build a house next door to that of the monks of Norwich, having first obtained the leave of the lord of the tenement, the Abbot of Malmesbury, under the common seal. In consideration for this license he promised the perpetual prayers of his abbey on behalf of the living and dead of the Abbey of Malmesbury. Half of this building he completed before his death. He also provided planks of "Eastland board" and other material for the completion of the same work.

The cost of the building during his abbacy was £138 3s. 2d. Within that period the common chapel of the houses, which has generally been known as John Whethamstede's chapel, was begun, and he contributed 100s. to this work. It is not surprising to hear that the monastic chroniclers of St. Albans thought he had spent *ultra debitum* on the work, and it is certain that he ran the Abbey into debt, an interesting commentary on the reputed wealth of the monastic houses. In order to meet the special expenses of this work and of other works in which he was engaged, the tithes of the rectories of Appelton Ridale in Yorkshire, Winslowe, and Bacheworth were devoted towards the house of the Abbey at Gloucester College.

Of his successor, William Heyworth, we know little, save that he continued the work of his predecessor, and made "the house of St. Albans finer than any other house in Gloucester College." The tithes of Appelton Ridale, amounting to £20 a year, which had been in arrears for six years, were again appropriated to the work. It is a thoroughly characteristic piece of mediæval economy. Whenever money was urgently needed for any purpose, it was the common practice to supply it by assigning a particularly bad debt to meet the expense. That the plan was found effectual there is good reason to believe, for it formed an integral part of finance even in the Government departments up to the beginning of the eighteenth century. On the whole work during this abbacy more than £165 was spent, besides the 20 marks expended in the preceding abbacy. On the other hand, the chapel and porch were paid for by a new scheme of voluntary contributions. The *decedentes* (the fifteenth-century parallel of the modern phrase "going down") subscribed to the purpose, and among those who gave donations were William Wyntersulle, John Whethamstede, and John Ysa. It was during this period that John of Whetham-

ST. ALBANS AND GLOUCESTER COLLEGE 45

stede was Prior studentium at Gloucester College, and to this fact we can trace the almost paternal interest he ever afterwards took in the affairs of the College.

According to some accounts John of Whethamstede came straight from Gloucester College to govern the monastery of St. Albans. The record of his first abbacy is very rich in references to Gloucester College, but unfortunately they are for the most part undated, and the simplest course is to deal with the history of the buildings during his abbacy—a history which is probably confined to the first few years after 1421, and then to deal with his other relations to the College. In this respect he completed the work of his predecessors, and has obtained the whole credit for it. He made one library for the whole Order, the building marked A in Loggan's sketch, which forms the frontispiece of this volume. We are told that he wrote, or caused to be written, for the monks of the monastery and those in the studium more books than any other Abbot since the first foundation of the Abbey. Their number was eighty-seven. He gave

"goode quantity of his owne study, and especially those of his owne composition, which were not a few, and to deter plagiaryes and others from abusing of them præfixt these verses in the front of every one of the same books, as he did also to those that he gave to the publick library of the University:

"'Fratribus Oxoniæ datur in munus liber iste
Per patrem pecorum prothomartyris Angligenarum :
Quem si quis rapiat raptim, titulumve retractet,
Vel Judæ laqueum vel furcas sentiat. Amen.'

"In other books which he gave to the said library these:

"'Discior* ut docti fieret nova regia plebi
Culta magisque Deæ datur hic liber ara Minervæ
His qui Diis dictis libant holocausta, ministris
Et Cirre bibulam sitiunt pre nectare limpham,
Estque librique loci, idem dator actor et unus.'†

"To him may be joyned Humphrey, called the good Duke of Gloucester, a monk of St. Albans,‡ who for his great love to learning and learned men did by the procurement of the said Whethamsted bestow many books to this library, as alsoe a worthy benefactor to many of his buildings in this college."

There is another entry as to the works of John Whethamstede, which gives rise to some doubt, and we will therefore give it in the original:

"Item in variis reparationibus apud Oxonias factis, ut puta in factura unius Librariae pro ordine, et in fabricatione cujusdam capellulae pro futuris monasterii studentibus ibidem, una cum clausura circa ipsorum gardinum expendit summam ultra centum et octo librarum."

The chief parts of this entry are plain enough: he built the library and the garden wall. But what is

* These lines are quoted from Wood. As they stand they cannot be translated. A suggested emendation is in l. 1. "Ditior" for "discior," "doctæ" for "docti," and the last line might run:

"Est librique locique, idem dator auctor et unus."

† One of these volumes has found its way into the library of Merton College, and is referred to as No. 318 in Coxe's "Catalogue of Oxford Manuscripts." It bears the first of the two legends quoted above. The volume, among other matter, contains a discussion of the important theological question whether "music can cast out devils."

‡ This statement is inserted on the authority of Wood. It is very doubtful.

meant by the *capellula?* The obvious answer is that it is the general chapel of the Order; but a closer investigation of the text gives rise to a surmise that he built a special small chapel, the use of which was confined to the monks of St. Albans. One must notice the antithesis between the " Library for the whole order," and then the little chapel for the monks of the monastery (the monastery, of course, being to a monastic chronicler the monastery of St. Albans). And all the other documents of the time to which we shall presently refer give colour to, though they do not confirm, this supposition. Exactly the same antithesis is to be noted in the account of the expenditure over these buildings, which for the same reason we will quote in full:

" EXPENSÆ CIRCA REPARATIONES.

" *Apud Oxonias.*

	li.	s.	d.
" Et in factura cujusdam Librariae pro communi Collegio Nigrorum Monachorum ibiden studentium	60	0	0
" Item in factura cujusdam capellulae ibidem ad usum monachorum monasterii pro tempore quo Prior studentium steterat	40	0	0
" Et in factura murorum circa gardinum ibidem	8	13	4
" Summa	108	13	4"

He also gave three silver saltcellars to his Oxford students, which cost £4, and subscribed £20 towards the building of the common chapel. Here again the expenses connected with the common chapel are kept distinct from those connected with the *capellula.* Lastly, we are told he built a vestiary adjoining to the chapel, in which the monks might put their vestments and other utensils.

Wood furnishes us with an account of John Whethamstede's chapel. He says it was built between the lower end of the hall or refectory and the clockhouse. It was dedicated to the memory of the father of the Order, St. Benet, and built about 1420 " by contributions from several bishops and abbots, and by supplication to them of Thomas de Ledbury, then prior of the house."

Amongst them John Whethamstede bestowed not only much cost towards the walls, but "alsoe the glasse windowes thereof," in which, especially the chief, he caused these deprecatory rhymes to be written under the pictures of the crucifix, the Virgin Mary, and St. John Baptist.

Under the crucifix were the verses:

"Mors medicina necis, via vite, pax populatus,
  Sis spes prompta precis, lex cure, laus monachatus."

Under the Virgin Mary were:

"Matris mesticia, mors prolis, vulnera quina
  Sint mea leticia, fati pulsante ruina."

Under St. John the Baptist were:

"Virginis imbutor, fidei fortissime tutor
  Nominis ut reputor feror omnis oro secutor."

Adjoining the chapel Abbot Whethamstede built a vestiary, and for these and other liberal acts to the College he was, on the motion of Edmund Kirton at a general chapter held at Northampton, pronounced to be the chief benefactor and second founder of the College.

Among other benefactors to the College we know that the monastery of Eynsham presented 20s. towards the building of the new chapel between 1414 and 1417; and it is also recorded that Sir Peter Besils, who built the bridge at Abingdon, was among the founders and benefactors, and that his arms were to be seen in the hall.

Having obtained for the College a library and for his students a chapel, the next step of John Whethamstede was to petition Pope Martin V. for leave to celebrate Mass in the chapel that was erected, and for this purpose to enjoy the use of a portable altar. The license is in all respects similar to that granted to the monks of Christchurch, Canterbury, during their temporary residence in Gloucester College in 1332, to which we have already referred. The only difference is that the monks of Canterbury thought it sufficient to obtain the leave of the Archbishop of Canterbury, while Abbot Whethamstede petitioned the Pope in person, a proceeding which was far more expensive.

It may again be noted here that the cost of obtaining the Bull, if it had been for the common chapel, would have been charged on the general funds of the whole Order, which were large, and not on the funds of St. Albans, as actually happened.

The bill for this particular Bull is still in existence. It should be noted that it does not include the expenses of the journey to Rome, but that it does include the expense of obtaining the same privilege for the house attached to the monastery in London.

"Bulla Altaris Portatilis.

Item, pro Minuta	10 florins.
Item, pro charta	3 bolonini.
Item, pro scriptore	10 florins.
Item, pro Bulla	11 florins.
Item, pro Registro	10 florins.
Item, pro clerico registrante	2 grossi.
Item, Clericis Domini Secretarii pro scriptura Minutarum	6 grossi.
Summa de moneta Anglicana	6*li.* 18*s.* 10*d.*"

The last effort of Abbot Whethamstede was directed towards the improvement of the condition of the students themselves. The whole story as told by John of Amundesham is so amusing and so characteristic both of John of Amundesham and the abbot, that we may be excused if we tell it at some length. John of Amundesham was himself, according to Bale, prior of the students at Gloucester College in succession to John Whethamstede himself. We can find no contemporary authority for the statement, and it is quite certain that if he was prior it was for an extremely short time, as there are a large number of letters addressed to the Prior of Gloucester Hall about this date, none of which bear his name, and Thomas Ledbury was apparently the successor of John Whethamstede. Whether this be so or not, there can be little doubt that he was a pupil, and a humble admirer of the great abbot whose history he writes. There is an almost ludicrous similarity of style in the writings of the two men. Each of them showed a considerable acquaintance with Scripture, each of them a great love

ST. ALBANS AND GLOUCESTER COLLEGE

for metaphor, and they were generally all the happier if the metaphors were slightly mixed. In each case horticulture was a strong point, and even here one finds the writers carried away by the exuberance of their fancy. John of Amundesham in one place makes the abbot go into his garden in the early spring and express the greatest surprise that the apples were not ripe, while the abbot whom he imitated compares the Bishop of Lincoln in turn to a sleeping dog, to a dropsy which becomes all the thirstier the more it drinks, and to a wolf among lambs. To return to the chronicle of John of Amundesham, it is related that in the spring of 1435 the Abbot of St. Albans visited the cell of Beaulieu in Bedfordshire, and found it "a barren figtree, which, having for three years borne no fruit, uselessly cumbered the ground." This is the account of John of Amundesham, but an unkind if more literal chronicler relates that the monks had got into trouble over the murder of a butcher. However this may be, the abbot cast about in his mind for a way to accomplish his purpose. He ascertained that it would be necessary first to get the permission of the founder of the cell. At a cost of £74 he bribed the friends of Lord Grey of Ruthin, the founder of the cell, to persuade him to consent to the change. After these preliminaries the consent of the lord was obtained in consideration of a certain annual number of prayers, that is to say, on March 16, 17, or 18 in each year they were to say a Placebo and a Dirige in the choir of the monastery, and a requiem Mass at the great altar on the following day. If ever they failed they were to pay 20s. by two half-yearly payments to Reginald

Grey, Lord of Ruthin, and his heirs. The first two steps being successfully accomplished, the abbot drafted a petition to Pope Martin V., in which he sought leave to disestablish the cell and devote the proceeds to the benefit of the monks of his *studium* at Oxford or at some other university. But this petition was abandoned, as the proctor at Rome said that the cost would be too great; so the abbot decided that he would dispense with a Bull, and he told the proctor to abandon his petition. With the funds he obtained from the disestablishment of the cell he increased the pension paid to his scholars. The task of paying for these prayers for the founder of the cell was allotted, curiously enough, to the "master of the works," an office established by Abbot Whethamstede, and he paid out in every year 53s. 4d. to each student of the Abbey at Oxford that he might pray for the soul of the founder, and for the souls of the father, uncle, and mother of the abbot. This is the entry in the ledger, but it is probable that 53s. 4d. is the sum total paid to all the scholars, for the extract from which it is taken is an estimate of the annual payments which the master of the works had to meet, and for this purpose it would be no use merely making an entry of the payment to a single scholar.

But the difficulties of the founder were not yet over. The King's Escheator came down and claimed that the cell of Beaulieu was forfeited, on the ground that the original founder was one of the King's ancestors, and that the later foundation of the cell of Beaulieu was a defiance of the statutes of mortmain. At this interesting point the narrative breaks off, and we have no

ST. ALBANS AND GLOUCESTER COLLEGE 53

means of knowing whether the abbot ever reaped the fruits of his immense expenditure.

Another interesting document of this period gives a very fair idea of the sums of money which were annually expended on the support of the chamber by St. Albans. The date of this document is about the end of the reign of Richard II. and the beginning of the reign of Henry IV.

The cook paid six pounds sixteenpence every year, the master of the refectory seven pounds, the master of the infirmary twenty-six shillings and eightpence, the camerarius a hundred shillings, the sacristan twenty-six shillings and eightpence, the almoner twenty-six shillings and eightpence, the under-master of the refectory five shillings, and the sub-almoner two shillings. These sums amount to twenty-two pounds, eight shillings, and fourpence. In addition to these charges paid by St. Albans itself, there were a number of sums paid by the various cells of the monastery for the support of students. The Prior of Tynemouth paid six pounds eight shillings, the Prior of Wymundham paid one hundred and four shillings, the Prior of Bynham paid fifty-three shillings and fourpence, the Prior of Belvoir paid thirty-two shillings and ninepence, the Prior of Walyngford paid thirty-one shillings and ninepence, the Prior of Hertford paid twenty-six shillings and eightpence, the Prior of Hatfeld Peverelle paid twenty-six shillings and eightpence, and the Prior of Beaulieu paid thirteen shillings and fourpence, making a total from these sources of twenty pounds, fifteen shillings, and sixpence, and a total for the whole Abbey of forty-three pounds, four shillings, and tenpence. To this must be added the two pounds, thirteen shillings, and fourpence which at a later date, as we have seen, was assigned to the students, and we get a total of forty-five pounds, eighteen shillings, and twopence—a very considerable sum in those days. We find in the cell of Beaulieu that eighteen pounds was considered sufficient to keep two monks, so this sum of forty-five pounds would be enough to keep five monks.

At a later date however (1480) there were only three monks at the studium at Oxford.

There are in existence five letters of Abbot Whethamstede written to, or in connection with, Gloucester College. Unfortunately, the abbot was one of those verbose letter-writers who always provided a pile of chaff for every grain of wheat, and but little information is to be derived from them. From internal evidence we gather that they are all dated in the first few years of his abbacy, and they are chiefly interesting owing to the evidence they afford of the constant troubles with which the College was disturbed, both internally and externally. In truth, the College did not seem to live in harmony at any period of its existence.

The first letter is of a pastoral character, addressed to the scholars at large. It is practically confined to telling the scholars to conduct themselves wisely, and to obey their Præpositus, a thing they were very much disinclined to do. Unfortunately, at exactly the point at which it seems likely that it might become interesting the scribe cuts it off with the abhorred shears of an "et cætera."

The second is perhaps the most interesting of the set. It is addressed to the Abbot of Malmesbury, and refers to the well-known and long-standing dispute as

ST. ALBANS AND GLOUCESTER COLLEGE

to the abbot's rights in the garden, meadow, and fishponds of the College. After a number of agricultural metaphors, it exhorts the abbot to do his best to remove the causes of discord in the College. As a compromise Whethamstede suggests that the Abbey of Malmesbury should abandon half its right to the said fishponds and meadow, in order to support the common houses of the College, and the abbot will in return remit the money which is due from Malmesbury to the general funds of the Order, and will, in addition, proclaim his munificence at the next general chapter of Benedictines.

The third letter is addressed to Thomas, Prior of Gloucester College. It says he has two things to concern himself with—the building of the chapel and the discipline of the students. As to the first he suggests that it is time the chapel was finished, and as to the second he says that the dissensions of the College have brought it into disrepute, and refers to the "childishness which, when it has a free rein, cannot confine itself within due limits, or abstain from the bitter apple of the forbidden tree." He then passes into a labyrinth of metaphors, referring in one paragraph to Abel, Cain, Martha, Mary, Rachel, Leah, Socrates, Aristippus, and Thersites.

The fourth letter is addressed to the scholars, and points to the pecuniary difficulties of the College. The contributions which they were receiving from the general Order were reduced at the moment when the rents of the Abbey were being reduced by ten per cent. It refers to the change in the value of the currency, and a reference to the great cost of original justice would lead us to suppose that it was penned at the time when he had exhausted his resources by bribing the friends of Lord Grey. Lastly, the abbot refers to the first-fruits he has been obliged to give the King. It ends up in a very kindly tone, telling the students to come home for their vacation, and he would pay any expenses they might incur as they enjoyed themselves on the way.

The fifth is a letter to the prior of the students, and chiefly relates to the chapel. It rather unkindly suggests that the only respect in which that edifice resembles the "Temple of Solomon" is that it has taken forty years building. The mention of Solomon suggests David, who was not thought worthy to build the Temple; then he suggests the Scriptural method in which people will revile the prior over the unfinished work, and expresses a hope that the building will not prove an "idea Platonis."

With the close of the life of John Whethamstede the record of the services rendered by St. Albans to Gloucester College comes to an end. It will be remembered that at the dissolution of the monasteries St. Albans was found to be one of those houses which were most in need of reformation, and no doubt the slackness of discipline in the parent house exercised a baneful influence on the students at the College.

CHAPTER IV

THE COLLEGE SYSTEM—EXPENSES OF THE BENEDICTINE STUDENTS—THE LAST YEARS OF THE COLLEGE—DISTINGUISHED MEMBERS OF GLOUCESTER COLLEGE

THE various rules which were drawn up for the regulation of the College give us considerable insight into its internal life, and these rules are supplemented by information obtained from various monastic accounts. It is plain that, though the abbots and priors of the monasteries were reluctant to send students to Oxford, the members themselves were eager and anxious to come. Not only was the life at Oxford far more enjoyable than in the comparative seclusion of the monasteries, but entrance into the College afforded the surest avenue to promotion, and a certain guarantee that the student would attain to the highest honours of the monastic world.

It is important to remember that the students sent to Oxford represented the pick of the Benedictine houses. A vacancy in the College for a student would occur very seldom, and we may be sure that the competition for the place was most eager. Even in the larger monasteries, where the vacancies were more common, the competition would be so much the keener. The

Benedictine Order was among the most learned Orders in England at a time when learning was still in a large degree the peculiar property of the monks and clergy. Out of this learned body the most promising members were selected to be educated at Oxford, and the student who took his degree after twenty years' training could fairly claim to be entitled to the highest positions in his Order.

To obtain the coveted honour of an election to Oxford the students resorted to every legal and illegal device. The elaborate rules drawn up by Benedict XII. for the selection of students bear witness to the importance which was attached to the matter. One in twenty of the members of every monastery or cell must go to a *studium generale*. If any monastery had less than twenty and more than eight members, it must send a student. A third clause is permissive. A monastery which had, *e.g.*, more than twenty but less than forty could send two members if it liked, unless there was something in its rules which compelled it to keep up its numbers at home. These rules remained unaltered throughout the history of the College, but there is every reason to suppose there were constant endeavours made to evade them. Only a few years later Benedict XII. found it necessary to call attention to the rule compelling a monastery with more than eight and less than twenty members to send a student. In some respects the rule was made more severe, since it was enacted that where a cell or monastery had more than six members, the visitors should inquire whether it could afford to send a student to College.

Most elaborate precautions were taken to secure the

sending of the most eligible pupils by the monasteries. The abbot or prior must, if he is the head of a cathedral body, select eight—if of an ordinary monastery four—monks, who are to be the electors of the students who are to go to Oxford. In order to decide they must consult the instructor, and both monks and instructor must be sworn to perform their office impartially. They must choose those who are apt to learn and of good morals. The students are to be selected for proficiency in theology and Canon Law, and of these, if possible, at least half must be students of theology. The electors are to be shut up in some separate place till the election has been made, an imitation of the procedure of the cardinals on the election of a Pope, and if they can come to no agreement, the abbot or prior has a casting-vote, which he must exercise within three days.

These rules were found to be sufficient till the days of Thomas de la Mare, but at that time, doubtless owing to the increased attractions of University life, a further rule was made enacting that old men must not be sent to College. The reason given is in curious opposition to the precepts of Aristotle. It was held that old men were not fit to understand philosophy.

Every possible precaution was taken to prevent a failure in the election. The head of the monastery was compelled to license the departure of the students, and if he refused to do so his second in command was bound to take his place. An abbot who failed to elect must pay a fine, and a failure to pay was successively followed by interdiction, suspension, excommunication, and deprivation. The last of these penalties was seldom, if ever, enforced. The fines received in this way were to be devoted to the College library. Thomas de la Mare added a law that the fine for a failure to send to the College should be £10 a year for each scholar, and if a scholar was kept away from College for a single term only a third of £10.

This was the legitimate way of getting admission to the College, but in the middle of the fourteenth century a practice grew up among the monks of getting the great men of the day to request admission for a favoured monk to the College, and this was doubtless linked with the bad practice of sending elder men who would have more influence. In the same way the Benedictine chapter was often canvassed. For instance, in 1340 it was ordered that the presidents of the chapter should write to the Prior of Rochester, the Abbot of Abingdon, and the Prior of Norwich, that they might allow certain of their members to take a course of either theology or Canon Law. Such requests were extremely inconvenient. The persons from whom they came were so mighty that they could not well be refused; while, on the other hand, they broke through the ordinary régime of election. So in 1349 it was enacted by Thomas de la Mare that no student should be allowed to canvass seculars in order to gain admission to the *studium* under pain of disqualification, and if he was already there at the time of the offence he was to be sent back. That the evil practice was not stamped out by this enactment is shown by its re-enactment in 1444, nearly a century later.

If the students were eager to come to College, their priors and abbots were proportionately unwilling that they should go. The prior of students had frequently to report some abbot to the chapter for failure to send his students, or for recalling them before their course was finished. In the chapter of 1342 fifteen abbots and priors were reported for their failure to send to the *studium*, and only two had any excuse to offer. In this case fines were inflicted according to the discretion of the presidents of the chapter. In 1426 the same complaint is made. Seven abbeys had failed to send the proper number of students. St. Augustine's, Canterbury, which ought to have sent four, had only sent two. Tavistock and Coventry had not sent any students at all for two years; Burton and Evesham had not sent any for three years. Others had failed to supply their students with money. In 1440 matters were much worse. Ten abbots had failed in their duty. The Abbot of Chester had not sent any students for twelve years, the Abbot of Abbotesbury had not sent any for seven years, and the Abbot of Michelney for six years. The Abbot of Hyde had "set a bad example to his brethren" by not sending his students any money for two years. The failure of the Abbot of Westminster was "all the more reprehensible because he lived in a peculiar and was the custodian of the regalia." The Abbot of Malmesbury had been "a constant offender," and deserved on that account the severest censure. Fines were imposed in due form, but there are signs of the weakness which was attacking monasticism when we find that, owing to continual clamour, the presidents "with their accustomed benignity" remitted the fines on promise of immediate reform.

There were abundant reasons why the abbots should

shirk the task of providing for their pupils, but the chief no doubt would be the expense involved. In all probability there was great emulation at the College itself between the various monasteries. The academical course at Oxford afforded innumerable opportunities for ostentation; this was inevitable when various monasteries were put in close juxtaposition to each other.

It is not easy to say with any certainty what would be the cost of supporting a student at Oxford. This cost might be divided into two branches—that which fell on the monasteries, and that which fell on the chapter. The law was definite enough as to the allowance which was to be paid by a monastery to a scholar. A scholar of theology who was not a master or a doctor (the terms are at this date synonymous) was to receive £10 per annum; a Doctor or Master of Theology was to receive £15 per annum. A scholar of Canon Law was to receive £8 15s. per annum, and a Doctor of Canon Law £12 10s. Mr. Anstey calculates that these sums may be multiplied by twenty in order to arrive at their value in modern money. Thus we find the largest class of scholars, the students of theology, would receive an average Oxford allowance of the present day, namely, £200 a year, and the other members of the college would receive some more and some less proportionately. The masters or doctors were unrestricted in their expenditure, but the scholars had certain parts of their funds allotted to certain purposes. Their ordinary expenses are to be £5 per annum; they are to spend 30s. a year on vestments and "calciaments," and the balance of 70s. was to be devoted to the purchase of books. If these payments were in any way adhered to, the Benedictine fared very much better than his secular contemporary. Whereas the Benedictine had £6 10s. to feed and clothe himself with, it is calculated that the average secular had about 51s. Moreover, the secular had to pay for the hire of his room, whereas the Benedictine probably was quartered free. But this was not the whole amount of his income. About the middle of the fourteenth century it was enacted that he should receive his travelling expenses, though if he came home without leave he was to forfeit them, and he seems to have been the only member of Oxford University of that day who made a practice of going home for the vacation. It is true that other students occasionally left Oxford for the vacation, but when they did so they often spent their time begging, while the Benedictine was received into the arms of his monastery. Of course this was almost necessary, otherwise during a long year's residence at Oxford the monk would almost forget that he belonged to any monastery at all.

In addition to the ordinary allowance the Benedictine received certain allowances on saints' days and festivals. We have seen how much the monks of St. Albans at Oxford enjoyed in this way. Another instance is afforded by the monks of Abingdon. The various officers of this Abbey invariably contributed something towards the expenses of celebrating the feast of the patron saint, Saint Edmund, at Oxford. In 1375 the treasurer gives 1s. 8d., in 1383 2s., and in 1440 6s. 8d. for a gaudy on the feast-day. The sacristan gives 3s. 4d. in 1396; the chamberlain gives a like sum in 1417 and 1428; the master of the refectory gives 1s. in 1422, and the gardener gives 2s. in 1450. It is probable that each of these payments was annual, otherwise one cannot understand how they should fall to different offices in different years, and the total received by the two fortunate students on St. Edmund's Day was probably considerable enough to enable them to feast the whole College. Provision was even made for oblations. The chapel-wardens gave them 4s. for offertories in the year 1466, but in 1469 nothing. That we hear little at Abingdon about the regular pension is doubtless due to the fact that some special source of income was appropriated to meet this expense, and the matter would not appear in the ordinary accounts of the Abbey. There are only two entries, neither of them complete. In 1383 the treasurer pays to the students £11 2s. 8d. in full payment of their pension, presumably for the year, but the rest they were to receive from the chamberlain, cellarman, refectorer, and the customary offerings, and in 1375 the sum of 75s. was paid for the half-year. There are a few similar entries with reference to the Abbey of Bury St. Edmunds. As early as 1299 we find:

"Comp. lib. magistris Oxon pro decima decime xl*s.* x*d.*
   qua.
Item eisdem. pro incepcione anno preterito omisso c*s.*"

In 1369-70 there was an allowance from this Abbey of x*s.* to three scholars at Oxford, and a number of payments were made in subsequent accounts for scholars at Oxford. In 1429-30 3s. 4d. was paid for a horse taking one scholar to Oxford, and in 1537 6s. was paid "in supplementum trium scholasticorum Oxon." The

From a photograph by the]   *[Oxford Camera Club*

NORTHERN BUILDINGS, FROM THE FELLOWS' GARDEN
(ABINGDON AND WESTMINSTER CHAMBERS)

Plate V

officiarii contributed £13 6s. 8d. to Edmund Brounfelde "qui incepit in Theol. Oxon, 1373." The various shrine keepers paid 10s. apiece, and the other obedientiaries other sums, when degrees were taken at the University by members of the Abbey, and we find this sum paid in 1520 to Edward Rowham, "pro gradu doctoris theologie suscipiendo secundum antiquam consuetudinem," with 6s. 8d. added by the prior's order. Lastly, the reversion of the manor of Pakenham was left to the Abbey "in elargitionem portionis monachorum predictæ abbatiæ Oxoniæ studentium." But we cannot draw from these figures any conclusion as to whether the full pension was ordinarily paid.

The method of raising these payments varied in different monasteries. In every case they had to be collected on a certain day, and paid over to the collector of the Benedictine Order, and from them they found their way to the students. Thus there was a direct guarantee that the provisions of the constitutions were enforced. The monasteries were ordered by Benedict XII. to assign certain perpetual payments to meet these charges. There is some reason to suppose that this order was at first—at any rate in respect to the greater number of the monasteries—ineffectual, for it is clear that in 1396 many monasteries had hitherto failed to perform this duty. We only know in a few cases what rents were appropriated to the scholar's pension. At Worcester the rent of Blackwell supplied the scholars with "ale, fewell, and other necessaries," and from this source £6 was paid to "every one of them." But other payments were received at the same house from other sources: 30s. was received from the Abbot of Osney out of Bybery Church. This came into the hands of the master of the kitchen, and supplied them with meat, while the chamberer received 30s. for their commons and other necessary duties, from what source is not stated. At Gloucester the tithes of Chipping Norton, amounting to 15 marks per annum, were devoted to the support of the students at Oxford in 1301, and the obit of Walter Frouceter, the Abbot of Gloucester, was celebrated at Oxford by a payment of a mark to the three or four Gloucester students at the place. In the same way the St. Albans students were endowed with the tithes of Beaulieu, Bacheworth, and Appelton Ridale.

It will have been noticed what a large proportion of his annual income the Oxford student was required to spend on books. In this respect he must have been far better provided than the ordinary student of that day, who was generally bookless. Certain fines were to be spent on books, and it is clear that there must have been a goodly collection in the College library. Students were forbidden to sell books, and they were not "even allowed to pawn them" to the University, which used constantly to lend money on the security of manuscripts. Thus the College as far as possible rendered itself independent of the University chests, which were kept in St. Mary's. If any monastery had more books than it wanted, or a number of duplicates, it was to distribute them after first making a note of the quarter in which the books were dispersed.

The student out of his pension was required to give certain sums to the prior. If there were less students than sixty they were to give the prior 5s. apiece; if they were more than sixty they were to give him £20 per annum altogether. But in 1444 the allowance of the prior was apparently reduced. The students were to give him 1s. 8d. each. Thus it would require 240 students to make up the old allowance of £20 a year.

In course of time it was found that the monasteries were extremely unwilling to retain their students at Oxford till they took their degree, and not only was the period required immoderately long, but the expenses of the degree were often immense, amounting sometimes to two or three years' ordinary income. It was the policy of the Benedictine chapter to encourage the taking of degrees, which " redounded to the credit and honour of the whole Order." So it was ordered that the inceptors should receive a gratuity out of the whole funds of the whole Order. An inceptor in theology was to receive £20, while an inceptor in Canon Law was to receive 20 marks (about £13); but it was enacted in 1343 that there must not be more than one of these payments in any one year. Thus, if there were two inceptors in theology they were to divide the money between them, and likewise with inceptors in Canon Law. In 1444 these laws were re-enacted and amended. If there was one inceptor in a year he was to have £20, and if there was more than one, each one was to have £10. Students of Canon Law were to have the same number of marks. A chest with three keys was established in the College to hold the funds which were to answer this purpose. One key was to be in the hands of the prior of students, another in those of the Abbot of Abingdon, and the third in the hands of the student with whom the chest was kept. £80 was to be put in the chest, and this ought to be sufficient to last from chapter to chapter, an interval of three years. A month before the inceptor took his degree he was to collect the three keepers of the keys and get his money out, and the keepers of the keys were to require the general collector of the Order to replace them. There was no subject on which the Benedictines felt so keenly as that a Benedictine must only study theology under a Benedictine. In the early days of the Order Doctors of Theology were very scarce. Of course the first doctor had no doctor under whom he could incept, so we find that the Chancellor of the University was his master on this important occasion. The first doctor was William de Brok, and when Laurence de Honsom, the second doctor, took his degree, William de Brok came on purpose from Gloucester, of which he was abbot, to preside at his inception. In 1340 this difficulty was avoided by an ordinance that any Doctor of Theology must remain at the College after taking his degree till another doctor came up to take his place. At the same time Thomas de Calton, a monk of Shrewsbury, was appointed Doctor of Theology, to continue in office till another could succeed him. Three years later it was ordered that a doctor remaining in this way at Oxford to teach the students was to receive £10 a year out of the common funds of the Order. In 1444 a new code was drawn up, and a fresh difficulty provided against. If any doctor was selected to take the chair of theology at the College, his abbot must allow him to come under a penalty of £10. Students were strictly forbidden to attend the lectures of an alien master when there was a properly qualified master in the house under pain of losing their pensions. In the same way they must not confess to anyone except a member of their own Order, and preferably to the prior of students.

The jurisdiction of the Chancellor's court was as far as possible excluded. Thomas de la Mare forbade anyone to plead before the Chancellor, but the prior must decide disputes. There was an ultimate appeal to the chapter. This was re-enacted in 1444 with the provision added that the prior might adopt four or five of the older students as assessors.

The position of the prior was one of exceptional difficulty. As has been already pointed out, the monastic was stronger than the collegiate spirit at Oxford, and the prior must have at times found the greatest difficulty in exerting his authority over the students of a monastery to which he did not belong. There are constant references in all the papers relating to the College to the difficulties and disorders with which the prior had to cope, though there is no positive information as to the actual character of these disorders. The constitutions of Abbot de la Mare refer specifically and pointedly to the dissensions and disorders in the society, and they state that the priors have been negligent or remiss in performing their duties.

It was doubtless these disorders which caused an alteration in the system under which priors were elected at first. The prior was appointed by the Abbot of St. Peter's, Gloucester, and presented to the founder, John Giffarde; then the election was put in the hands of the students themselves, as would have been the case in an ordinary priory. In the later years of the founder's life the nomination was either transferred to Malmesbury Abbey or the appointment was vested solely in the founder. He exercised this right in 1299 by appointing a nameless monk of Malmesbury to the office of Prior studentium. There is reason to suppose that the Abbot of Malmesbury claimed the office of prior for his senior student at the College, who was thus independent of the ordinary prior studentium. After the founder's death the election was transferred, according to the democratic principles of the Benedictine Order, to the general body of students. This system could not but produce disorder in the election and want of discipline in the government of the College. Local feeling in those days was extremely keen, and we can imagine that the election must often have produced a state of anarchy. The statutes of Benedict XII. introduced an entirely new element into the government of the College. The President of the Order was to appoint some abbot belonging to a monastery close at hand, who should exercise general supervision over the students. This duty was entrusted to the Abbot of Abingdon, who appears to have held the office corresponding to that of visitor perpetually. The Abbot of Abingdon was to appoint a prior. There is no definite information that any alteration was ever made in this rule throughout the history of the College, but it is curious that we do not hear of any case in which the Abbot of Abingdon intervened in the affairs of the College, and there is a rule of 1444 which certainly suggests that at some unknown time the College reverted to the system of popular election. It was ordered that there should be no canvassing for the office of prior; anyone who canvassed was to be disqualified from holding office. It was added that the practice of canvassing had caused great disorder in the past. It is not easy to see how canvassing a single person such as the Abbot of Abingdon could cause great strife and scandal in the Church. The same clause suggests that the Presidents of the Order should nominate suitable candidates to stand for the office.

The changes in the office were extremely frequent. Without doubt it would nearly always be the senior student who would be appointed Prior studentium, and his early retirement from Oxford would cause a vacancy. In the last years of the College we find there were three elections in the course of five years, and if tradition is correct, there were at least six priors in a space of less than thirty years at the beginning of the fifteenth century.

The prior was the general disciplinary officer of the College. He was the medium by which the College communicated with the Benedictine chapter and the outside world. He could exercise powers of correction, supervise the expenditure of the students, recommend the proficient to the chapter in order that they might be continued at Oxford, and report the idle that they might be recalled. He was the custodian of the College buildings so far as they did not belong to any particular monastery, and his perpetual anxiety was to obtain the necessary funds to keep these buildings in order. He had to perform the unpleasant duty of reporting those Abbots who failed in their duty to the College to the general chapter, and this task must have been peculiarly unpleasant in a case where he had to report his own abbot or the Abbot of Abingdon, who elected him. He was the official representative of the College in the University, and he had to hold his own court to decide disputes between the students. He could absolve the students from any general sentence of excommunication which had been issued against their abbey or the University. In addition to these arduous tasks, he had some educational functions to perform.

The priors varied very considerably in energy and in the part they played in the University. The position of the College and the general dislike for the monastic orders probably prevented the Prior of Gloucester College occupying any prominent position in the affairs of the University. However, we know that at least two held the office of Commissary or Vice-Chancellor— namely, Richard Ringstede and Robert Ixworth. But if their position made them unpopular, their wealth made them influential. Above all others, Edmund Kirton, who was prior about 1426, put the University under a heavy debt of gratitude. In 1426 the University, which was at the time afflicted with chronic poverty, wrote a letter to the Benedictine chapter requesting assistance in the construction of the theological schools. It referred in the most flattering terms to the fact that our "alma mater," the University, "owed its fortunate beginning and its most fortunate progress to the excellent fathers of the holy Benedictine Order." In conclusion, it expressed a hope that the prior, Edmund Kirton, would take the degree of Doctor of Theology as a fitting climax to an unusually splendid

Oxford career. Edmund Kirton was the doctor selected to carry this letter to the Benedictine chapter. It was not the first time they had rendered assistance to the University in its need. They had already granted £100 towards the repair of the University church, and now they voted a notable sum to meet the needs of the University. We do not know what the sum actually granted was, but in 1430 there is an acknowledgment of 50 marks in part payment of £100. And on April 27, 1431, the University acknowledged in a graceful letter what was apparently the balance due, and promised that the scholars of the Order should have the same rights, privileges, and use of the new schools as was enjoyed by seculars. Apparently a fresh grant was made a little later, for in 1444 the University writes to say that it has received the first part of a promised donation, and is sending its proctor to collect the rest, as they are in immediate need of money for the new schools.

At a later date the University was able to repay the service that Edmund Kirton had done it. When he was at Basle in 1437 he was imprisoned on a charge of heresy, and only released on the active intervention of the University of Oxford and the Duke of Gloucester.

The relations of the University and the College in the matter of the schools afforded one more reason why it behoved the College to conciliate the University. Oxford was never inclined to be very lenient to the regular Orders. It made them pay for such privileges as they possessed. We can best understand the relations if we take the career of a typical student of the College.

He would come up to Oxford at the age of nineteen or twenty. Originally the University insisted that every person who took a Theological degree should first take the degree of Master of Arts, and lecture at one time for a period of one year, at another for a period of two years, in the schools as Regent Master of Arts. But exemptions from this stringent rule were constantly granted to the regular Orders; in fact, some of the monastic Orders were prevented by their constitution from reading Arts at all. These exemptions, from being matters of favour, became in time matters of course, so much so that a refusal to grant such an exemption caused the gravest disorder in the University. At length in 1421 it was decided that in future the members of the regular Orders should be exempted as a matter of course from taking the Arts course. We do not know how far the Benedictines availed themselves of this privilege. We know, for instance, that Richard of Wallingford, who lived to be the Abbot of St. Albans, took the full Arts and Theology course; and it is likely that, for the credit of the Order, the Benedictine student received some training in Arts before he proceeded to the higher degree. At the opening of his career at the College he had two courses open to him. He could read either Canon Law or Theology. The first was less profitable and less troublesome than the second. The student had to study the Civil Law for three years, and at the end of this period he would attend lectures on the Decretum of Gratian for two years and on the Decretals of Gregory IX. and Boniface VIII. for three more. Thus, at the end of eight years he became a Bachelor of Canon

Law. With this degree he had more authority than a Bachelor of Arts. He was allowed to lecture, and after a reasonable period he would proceed to his Doctor's or Master's degree. Some trouble was caused owing to the fact that the Bachelors of Canon Law claimed to occupy the same precedence as Masters.

The theological student had a much harder course. The rules of his monastery ordered him to study theology for six years before he began to read the Bible, which was the commencement of the theological course at Oxford. Then a three years' course of Bible reading followed. In his fourth year at Oxford the student was allowed to oppose in the disputations which were held in the schools. After two years of this course, he was permitted to respond—whence the modern name "responsions" is derived—and shortly afterwards he was allowed to determine. Determination always began at Oxford on the morning of Ash Wednesday, and ended ten days before Easter. The period was spent in arguments and disputes in the schools, and when it was finished the student was allowed to take his degree as Bachelor of Theology. Among the seculars this was an occasion of feasting and merriment; but the Benedictine, perhaps because the period of determination always fell in Lent, was forbidden to celebrate his determination with a feast. From the time he became a Bachelor he was allowed to lecture.

His first course was on the sentences of Peter Lombard, his second on the Bible. Then he had to attend eight disputations held among the Bachelors, and preach a probationary sermon in Latin in St. Mary's, and at length he was allowed to become a Master or Doctor of

Theology. The assumption of the degree was celebrated with magnificent festivities, though they were not so great as those among the seculars. He was bound to swear that he would not spend more than £27 15s. 6d. in English money over his inception, whereas the secular was only limited to £41.

We have a lively account of the great occasion when the first Doctor of the Benedictine Order took his degree. In 1298, on the morrow of St. Barnabas, William de Brok, a monk of Gloucester, celebrated his inception in theology under Richard de Clyve, the Chancellor of the University. At his Vesperiæ Laurence de Honsom, a member of the society, answered the question which he propounded. The Abbot of Gloucester was present, with his monks, priors, obedientiaries, clerks, esquires, as also an hundred noblemen and esquires that came with them, all horsed. Thither also came the Abbots of Westminster, Reading, Abingdon, Evesham, and Malmesbury, together with many priors and monks. They all gave the inceptor various presents, and the abbots and prelates of the Order throughout the whole province of Canterbury who were not present sent presents by their representatives. "And so the inception was celebrated to the honour of this house and the whole Order."

On the occasion of the Vesperiæ a dinner was given to the regent masters of the faculty, and the bedels would be presented with 20s. and a pair of gloves. The inceptor, according to his means, would distribute presents of robes among his fellow-students and the masters under whom he had read. On the morrow he would be formally admitted in St. Mary's Church before a master

THE COLLEGE SYSTEM

of his own Order, who was called his father. He received a cap, book, a golden ring, and the kiss of peace, and he was henceforth entitled—in fact, compelled—to lecture as a Doctor of Theology. He would remain at the College for one year to lecture, and perhaps if he was required to teach the students he would remain longer. During this time he preached a Latin sermon in St. Mary's. And so he would return to his monastery a man marked for the first promotion that offered itself. By the statutes of the Order he was to take precedence before all the officials of his monastery except the abbot and the priors of cells or the sub-priors of cathedrals.

Towards the close of the fifteenth century the feast was sometimes abandoned. In 1537 the monks of Gloucester College made an agreement with the bedels as to this matter, which is somewhat obscure. The University bedels at an inception occupied a somewhat similar position at that time to that held by undertakers at a funeral. The arrangements of the inception were in their hands, and they delivered the invitations. Each of the monks at Gloucester agreed to pay to the bedel of his faculty 1s. 8d., and within eight days after the payment the bedels undertook to provide a goodly breakfast, dinner, or supper; but in future years the monks might either pay 1s. 8d. and have the supper, or 1s. 4d. and abandon the supper. Bachelors of Theology, however, were to pay 3s. 4d. a year, with an allowance of 4d. if they agreed to abandon the supper. By a supplementary agreement in 1538 the students undertook to pay half the proper sum on St. John the Baptist's Day and the other half at Michaelmas.

Though the ordinary student at Gloucester College undoubtedly aspired to a degree, it is plain that a great many went away without obtaining one. Provision is made for philosophical students, who must study under the prior in such a way as not to interfere with lectures in the schools. It is stated that some of the students came chiefly in order that they might learn how to preach, and such were to dispute twice a week in each branch of study. They must preach frequently both in English and Latin. The logical and philosophical course was to be as John of Whethamstede ordered. There must be sermons at least four times a year, and certain days were selected as being most suitable for this purpose. From these and similar provisions it is clear that there was a regular system of teaching inside the College under the prior and the Doctor of Theology as well as in the schools. Practically the whole of the Benedictine's education was in the hands of members of his own Order, and any deviation from this rule occasioned a great disturbance. In 1359 H. de Wodehull, in order to escape the heavy fees that were exacted from Benedictines, attempted to incept under a. secular, and thus excited the grave displeasure both of his Order and of the University.

During all the years in which Gloucester College existed it is probable that it had next to no history to disturb its monastic life. Certainly we have been able to glean only a few facts from the past. The rest would be a record of inceptions and determinations, feasts and fasts, visitations and contentions.

But perhaps the College never held so prominent a place in the affairs of the world as on the occasion of

THE COLLEGE SYSTEM 79

the visit of the Archbishop of Canterbury in 1379. The news that he was about to visit Gloucester College created something like a panic. Reason told the monks that contention would help them not at all against so vigorous a prelate. So they resolved to resort to stratagem. The Abbot of Westminster took counsel with the Abbot of St. Albans, "one of the most respected abbots" of the day. It was decided to send for the prior of students in haste the day before the visitation to take counsel with his abbot on the affairs of the monastery. The letter should be handed to the prior at the hour of vespers so that the fact should be notorious. He was to set forth at once and appoint a proctor in his absence. When the Archbishop or his deputy came to hold the visitation and called for the prior, he would be informed by the proctor that the prior was away, but the proctor would be careful to conceal the fact of his appointment. If the excuse was accepted, the visitation would be abandoned, and by the time the prior returned the writ would have expired. If the Archbishop's messenger swore that the prior had received the writ, the students present must swear the opposite. If further objections were raised, the proctor was to produce the letter summoning the prior away as his trump card. This in brief was the plan of action for the first day. They prepared another plan of action for the second day, but as it was not needed in the events which happened, we are left in doubt as to its nature. At the same time the Abbot of St. Albans wrote to the Archbishop asking him to abandon the visitation. A messenger was sent. The Archbishop received him "with a cheerful countenance," and asked

him to dinner. After dinner he assured the messenger
that he would do anything he could for the abbot in
reason, but he could not abandon this visitation *salvo
jure ecclesiæ suæ.* The College had all the peculiarities
of a place to which his powers extended. It was a
college, its members lived in common, and its prior
could hold a chapter. The messenger replied that it
was not a college because it had not got a corporate
seal and was not endowed. The Archbishop replied
very pertinently that he would come and see whether
that was the case. "But," said the monk, "you have
no jurisdiction. You cannot visit such of the monks
as belong to monasteries which are exempt from jurisdiction, and the rest have already been visited in their
own monasteries, and you cannot visit them again."
The Archbishop replied that when he went to the
monasteries he was told to come to the College, and
when he went to the College he was told to go to the
monasteries. An expert lawyer added that he could
visit the exempt monks also, not as monks, but as
scholars under the jurisdiction of the Chancellor of
Oxford. The reply was that if they were exempt anywhere they were exempt everywhere. And the Archbishop gave way, saying that he did not wish to trouble
them if that was the case. On St. Brice's day the prior
appeared before the Archbishop, and begged him to
abandon his visitation, but he refused. However, soon
afterwards the prior and all the monks marched down
to St. Frideswide after sunset and appeared before the
Archbishop, who construed this as a sign of submission.
But the prior replied that they had not come to submit,
but to win his favour. The Archbishop replied: "I

hold you excused; I do not intend to burden you." And so the attempted visitation ended.

On reading such a story as this one may discredit the honesty—one certainly cannot impugn the diplomacy—of the Benedictine Order. Other incidents were of a most trifling description. In 1377 Roger Marchal, John Dunwych, John Bacle, Stephen Holsoye, John Frasthorp, Thomas Norton, John Manston, and William Whetle entered the house of the monks of Gloucester in the suburbs of Oxford, and feloniously broke into the chamber of one Brother Mylys, a monk of Glastonbury, and stole therefrom £7 5s. 8d. in gold and silver. We do not know what happened to these mediæval burglars, but the incident is curious as showing the large sum of money possessed by a monk of the day.

Towards the middle of the fifteenth century there are signs of the growing irregularity of monastic life. It was found necessary to order monks to haunt the taverns "less than had been their wont," and to forbid them to spend the night out. In 1452 William Ellismere, a scholar of Gloucester College, was summoned before the Chancellor, and convicted along with a fishmonger and others of a breach of the peace. They wandered through the whole of the parish of St. Aegidius carrying arms, and beat a certain labourer called John Laws, and robbed a smith of a "glena" which he carried with him. Later on the same memorable evening the disorderly gang had gathered together scholars and others, and beaten a tailor, J. Wodestok, and had robbed a scholar of Aristotle Hall of his hood, which was worth 6s. 8d. We are fortunately left in doubt as to the ultimate fate of this versatile criminal.

But the Gloucester College student went from bad to worse. We seem to see his downward career in the record of 1517, in which the University tells Cardinal Wolsey "how one John Haynes had armed four turbulent Benedictines and three seculars and endeavoured to kill a proctor."

About this time the State Papers begin to heap up accusations against the College. "Horman Men, a bookseller of Oxford, confesses to having eaten in the Lent of 1539 twenty legs of mutton, five rounds of beef, and six capons, and a black monk of Canterbury or Gloucester College" is said to have joined with him in this reprehensible practice. In 1534 Richard Croke writes to Cromwell in great indignation at the monks and "other ignorant religious persons."

"You have probably seen" (said he) "the device intended to have been played in Gloucester College, a place of monks, if Mr. Carter had not stopped it. The Commissary has the said play. You will not believe how the monks and canons and all other ignorant religious persons, enemies to the King's cause, rejoiced at the stay of the works and College."*

The unhappy monks were as powerless to escape from ridicule as they were from popular hatred. An instance is afforded by the celebrated alarm of fire at St. Mary's, the University church, in 1536. The alarm was a false one, but such was the press of people running

* The College, of course, was Cardinal College, afterwards Christchurch.

in heaps together that the more they laboured the less they could get out. And

"here there happened a pageant in a certain monk, if I be not misadvised, of Gloucester College, whereat Calphurnius might well laugh with open mouth. It happened that there was a young lad in this tumult, who, seeing the doors fast stopped with the press or multitude, climbed up on the door, and there stayed, for he durst not come down. And it so happened that among those that got out over men's heads he saw a monk coming towards him who had a great wide cowl hanging at his back. When the monk came near unto him the boy came down, and prettily conveyed himself into the cowl. At last the monk got out over men's heads with the boy in his cowl, and for a great while felt no weight or burden. At last, when he was somewhat more come to himself and did shake his shoulders, feeling his cowl heavier than it was accustomed, and also hearing the voice of one speaking behind, he was more afraid than he was before when he was in the throng, thinking in very deed that the evil spirit which had set the church on fire had flien into his cowl. By-and-by he began to play the exorcist. 'In the name of God,' said he, 'and all saints, I command thee to declare what thou art that art behind my back.' To whom the boy replied: 'I am Bertram's boy, good master; let me go;' and with that the cowl began to crack with the weight. The monk, when he perceived the matter, took the boy out, and the boy took to his legs, and ran away as fast as he could."

Curiously, too, the jest of the shrewd observer who wondered how there were any Englishmen left in England, because there they burnt Papists and anti-Papists at the same fire, was justified in the case of Gloucester

College, for we find it connected closely with the case of Garret, the distributor of heretical literature. The matter has already been referred to in this series in the "History of Lincoln College," and it is fully recounted in the "Acts and Monuments of John Foxe." So we will refer to it but briefly.

About 1528 one Garret, a London curate, came to Oxford to distribute Protestant literature. It is interesting to find among his patrons Anthony Delabere, a scholar of St. Alban Hall, who subsequently moved to Gloucester College, though he was a secular. Garret took refuge with him, borrowed his coat, and made his way into the country. That night Delabere slept at St. Alban Hall, but he came back to College at five o'clock the next morning, and was soon afterwards summoned by the prior, Anthony Kitchin, to explain his part in the affair. During his absence the officers of the University had entered his chamber and ransacked the room for any traces of Garret. Presently all were summoned before the Chancellor at Lincoln College, and as Delabere's answers were unsatisfactory he was put in the stocks, his feet as high as his head, while his examiners went off "unto their abominable mass." Eventually Garret was discovered in Somersetshire. Being brought back to Oxford, he was compelled to walk with Delabere, carrying a faggot, in open procession from St. Mary's Church to Frideswide. In course of time Garret was burned alive, but Delabere survived the horrors of the Marian persecution and died in 1562.

There were several other Gloucester men among the reformers of this period: one Eden, with others of

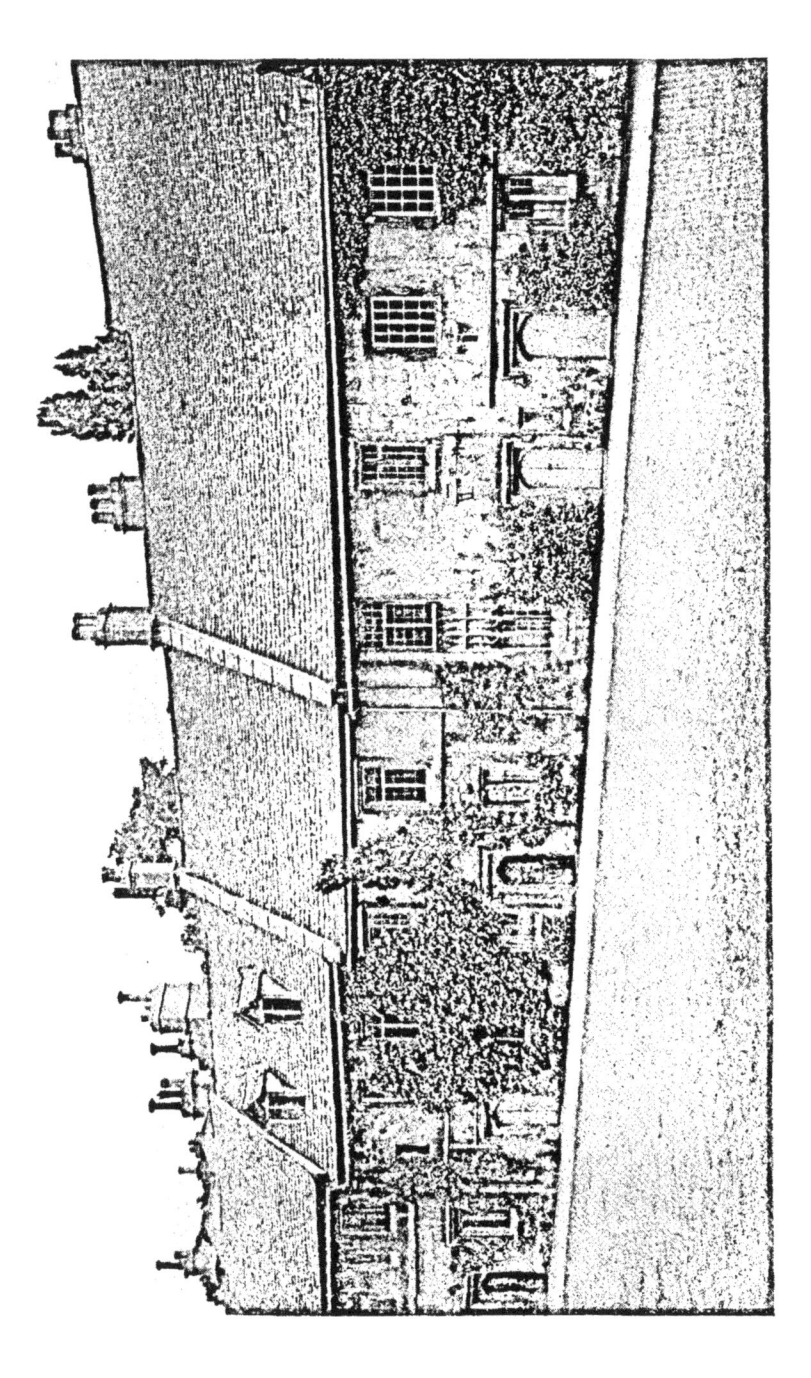

From a photograph by the [*Oxford Camera Club*]

SOUTH SIDE OF THE QUADRANGLE

Plate IV

Gloucester College, a monk of St. Edmondsbury, named John Salusbury, and a young priest of Sherborne, in Dorset, who was, at any rate, in secret sympathy with the reformers.

Under date 1517 Brian Twyne notes, but is unable to explain, a gift which connects the College with the building of Corpus, then in progress : "Item delivered to ye Prior of Students at Gloucester College by my lord's Command x*li*."

In 1539 we obtain the first suggestion of approaching dissolution. Philip, Abbot of Evesham, wrote on January 23 in that year to the students to inform them that he had commandment from "my Lord Privy Seal to make a governor of the College, and take the inventory of plate, furniture of the chapel, and other movables, and to send the same to him. I have therefore appointed your manciple the bearer to carry it up, and require you to permit him quietly to receive the same." In the following year the College came to an end, and its lands were granted to an alien holder.

We may conclude this long chapter with some mention of the great men Gloucester College has produced. No doubt the list would be a longer one if it was possible to say with more certainty of any Benedictine that he was a member of the College. Nearly all the names we can mention belong to the period just before the Dissolution, and it is interesting to see how that movement affected various members of the College.

John Feckenham was a native of the little Worcestershire village which was one day to receive the benefaction of our founder, Sir Thomas Cookes. He joined the Abbey of Evesham as a novice, and came up to

Gloucester College at the age of eighteen. Soon after his return to his monastery his abbey was dissolved (1535), and he returned to Gloucester College the recipient of a pension for life of 100 florins from the exchequer. He became chaplain to the Bishop of Worcester, and later to Bonner, the Bishop of London, whom he attended in the Tower of London during the reign of Edward VI. By his influence the Abbey of Westminster was refounded in 1556, and for two years he held the office of abbot of that house. He preached the funeral sermon on Queen Mary, and was committed to the Tower by Queen Elizabeth, whom he had often befriended. The rest of his life was passed in a progress from prison to prison, and he ended his days at Wisbech Castle in 1585. He was a man beloved by all parties, and it is said that Queen Elizabeth offered him the primacy on condition of his taking the oath of supremacy.

John Stanywell, at one time Prior of Gloucester College, was also one of the "last abbots." He was Abbot of Pershore and Episcopus Poletensis till the dissolution of the monasteries, when he retired into private life, dying in 1553 at a great age.

Very different were the fates of men like John Wakeman and Anthony Kitchin. The former was the last Abbot of Tewkesbury, but on the dissolution of his house in 1541 he became the first Bishop of Gloucester. The latter was the Vicar of Bray of the sixteenth century. He was a monk of Westminster, and became in succession Prior of Gloucester College and last Abbot of Eynsham. He received a pension of £133 on the dissolution of his house, together with the promise of a benefice. In 1545 he became the Bishop of Llandaff, and he was the only bishop who clung to his bishopric throughout all the changes that followed in the English Church. He burnt a martyr under Queen Mary, and took the oath of supremacy under Queen Elizabeth. He died Bishop of Llandaff at the age of eighty-six, and Wood refers with some acrimony to the way in which he wasted the property of the see: " A bad Kitchin did for ever spoil the good meat of the Bishops of Llandaff."

Among earlier members of the College we may mention two other Abbots of Westminster. Thomas Mylling, a monk of Westminster, who became abbot of that house in 1469. In that capacity he gave sanctuary to Elizabeth Woodville in 1470, and Edward V. was born in his house. He became Bishop of Hereford in 1473, an office which he held till his death in 1493. He was one of the earliest English scholars to study Greek. The other was Edmund Kirton, an energetic prior of the College and a very successful Abbot of Westminster.

Edmund de Bromfield, a monk of Bury St. Edmunds, was almost certainly a member of the College. He was promoted " usque ad summum gradum " at Oxford at the expense of his monastery; but whenever he was recalled he proved a source of discord. In consequence, he was sent to Rome, and there appointed Abbot of Bury St. Edmunds in defiance of the King in 1379. He was imprisoned for nearly ten years, but was released in 1389, and appointed Bishop of Llandaff.

Miles Salley, or Sawley, was a Benedictine of Abingdon, who came to the College, and, like Kitchin, became successively Abbot of Eynsham and Bishop of Llandaff (1504-1516). He was a benefactor to the University of Oxford.

A more humble member of the College proved fortunate at the dissolution of the house. This was Richard Gunter, the Manciple. Afterwards, "to use brewing," he was fain to become free of the town. He was Mayor of Oxford in 1545 and 1546.

We may also refer to Richard Kedermyster, Abbot of Winchcombe in 1487, and a great supporter of the rights of the minor orders of clergy, and John Lawerne, a theologian of Worcester, whose lectures, doubtless delivered by him as D.D. of Gloucester College, are now in the Bodleian.

There are two other men whom we should like to claim. It is generally stated that Thomas Walsingham and John Langdon, Bishop of Rochester, were members of the College. But the former was a Carmelite all his life, and the other was a monk of Christ Church, Canterbury, and, according to some accounts, Warden of Canterbury College. In any case, neither of them would be educated at Gloucester College.

Of John Lydgate, the poet, and disciple of Chaucer, who was a monk of Bury St. Edmunds, as Bale asserts that he studied at *both* the English Universities, it may be inferred—no more can be said—that he was a member of Gloucester College.

The names we have given are almost all that chance has preserved to us. They are probably fairly good examples of the lives of the more successful members of the College.

CHAPTER V

1541—1626

THE DISSOLUTION—THE BISHOP OF OXFORD'S PALACE—THE FOUNDATION AND PROGRESS OF GLOUCESTER HALL

As the monasteries which fed it were dissolved, the means of existence of the members of Gloucester College must have disappeared, together with all hopes of success in the career to which they had been destined. Under these circumstances they must rapidly have scattered, though a few perhaps lingered on and haunted the old buildings. The land was first dealt with in December, 1541, when there was a grant to John Glin and John James, Yeomen of the Guard, in survivorship of the "keeping or oversight of the mansion called Glocestre Colledge, without the suburbs of Oxford, late appertaining to divers religious houses now dissolved." Very soon afterwards John Glin was succeeded by John Ellis. At the same time another part of the College was dealt with by sale to Edmund Powell, of Sandford, who acquired a close containing three and a half acres, commonly called "Glocester College Close," and another containing two acres near it.

Edmund Powell was also the grantee of the Carmelite Priory on the other side of Stockwell Street, and he and his children were responsible in great measure for the demolition of that house. It may have been he who commenced the destruction of Gloucester College. However, these grants were for some reason withdrawn, and we next hear of Gloucester College as the proposed episcopal seat of the Bishop of Osney. The College was included in the formal grant of the temporalities of the See of Osney, dated September 1, 1542. The " parcels " were :

"All that college, mansion, or house of ours called Gloucester College, situate and being in the parish of St. Nicholas in our said county of Oxford, and outside the suburbs of our said city or town of Oxford, and situate and lying near our said Monastery of Osney, and also all and singular its houses, buildings, chambers (cameras), structures, gardens, meadows, and territories whatsoever situate, lying, or being within the site or precinct of the same college, house, or mansion of Gloucester College, or known by the name or names of Gloucester College, or the parts and members of the same so held or reputed to be held, and all the gardens and meadows to the said college, house, or mansion pertaining or belonging, and now or late in the tenure, custody, or occupation of John Ellys and John James, or their assigns, all which mansion and other premises called Gloucester College are of the clear yearly value of 26s. 8d., and no more, so that the said mansion, or house, and other premises commonly called Gloucester College, may henceforth be, and be regarded as and be called, the mansion, habitation, or palace of the above mentioned Bishop of Oxford, and his successors the Bishops of Oxford."

It is said that Robert King lived here from 1542 to June 9, 1545, when the see was removed to Christchurch. Though the necessary legal formalities were not completed in the reign of Henry VIII., Bishop King had gone so far as to assign all the temporalities of the see to Henry VIII., pending a new grant, but had not included Gloucester College in this assignment. When Edward VI. came to the throne, by a tripartite indenture, made January 15, 1548, between the King, Edward Duke of Somerset, and the executors of Henry VIII. and Robert King, the Bishop, the King covenanted to endow the bishopric according to the plan proposed by Henry VIII. Again Gloucester College was not mentioned. A nice variety of legal questions arose upon the construction of these various documents. Matters were complicated by a question as to which of the deeds had been enrolled in Chancery, a necessary preliminary in order to obtain security of title, as the Irish landlords of this date discovered to their cost. The matter dragged on, as is the way with legal questions, for about seventy years. Queen Elizabeth entirely disregarded the grant to King, and made a grant to William Doddington in 1560. The lands were then described as being of the clear annual value of sixty shillings. There is a full description here of the dimensions of the College:

"The site and circuit of the said College.

"Two buildings or lodgings upon the south and north part of the said College.

"Seven chambers, every one in length xvi foot, in breadth xii foot.

"Two other buildings upon the north part of the said

College, containing in length xx foot, in breadth xviii foot.

"The Hall, in length lx foot, in breadth 30 foot.

"Another building adjoining to the said Hall in length xx foot, in breadth xii foot.

"Six small lodgings adjoining upon the south part of the said Hall, whereof two beneath and iiii above, containing in length 30 foot, in breadth xvi foot.

"The base court, in length 80 foot, in breadth 60 foot.

"The soil of the late church, in length 40 foot, in breadth 20 foot.

"The ground within the site, in length 80 foot, in breadth 40 foot, upon which divers other lodgings were erected by John Williams, knight, lately wasted and fallen down.

"The garden and orchard.

"Two parcels of mead enclosed with water, whereof one containing ii acres, the other three acres."

The list is valuable, not only as enabling us to draw a ground-plan of the College as it stood, with the help of Loggan's sketch, but also because it gives us the only hint we receive as to the work of Sir John Williams, the well-known knight of Thame, in the College. We hear of him in connection with St. Mary's College as one who sold "timber and slatt" from thence to the city. He was the founder of Thame School, and builder of Botley Bridge.

Doddington bought the property, only to sell it again. Sir Thomas White, the founder of St. John's, purchased it from him on March 23, 1560. One of the pleadings recites that—

"for the like advancement of learning, he, redeeming the said dissolved College from utter ruin, did purchase the same from our late Sovereign Qº Elizabethe, and therein did erect a house of learning by the name of the Principall and Scholars of St. John's Hall."

A later pleading states that Sir Thomas White did bestow "great cost in re-edifying the buildings that were utterly decayed, and made it a house of students." Legend says that Sir Thomas White had originally fixed upon Gloucester Hall for the site of his College, but that he saw in a dream a tree that should mark the site of the foundation. Long he searched for it, till one day, riding by chance by St. Bernard's College, he recognised in a great elm, out of which grew three trunks, the tree of his dreams.

We may perhaps finish the history of the litigation. Neither Bishop King nor Bishop Curwen apparently took any trouble about the matter. Then there was a long vacancy in the see, and in 1590 John Underhill, Bishop of Oxford, revived the matter before Mr. Justice Windauer and Chancellor Hatton at the Oxford Sessions. To try his rights, "he did by his bailiff and others make an entry by night and by water, and did drive away the horses depasturing in the grounds belonging to the said Hall, impounding the two." No doubt further action was rendered impossible by the death of the Bishop in 1592, and an eleven years' vacancy of the see. The matter came up again in the suit of Thomas Bland *versus* Anthony Tythers and John Chambers. The defendants were the bailiffs of John Bridges, Bishop of Oxford. The plaintiffs complained that they, on May 31, "at the City of Oxford, in a place called Gloucester Hall Meadow, took four geldings of the plaintiffs, and them detained, etc., *ad damnum* 40*li*."

As was the case with the earlier suits, nothing came of it, and the Bishop took up his residence at March Baldon.

St. John's College must now have hoped for a season of peace; but no sooner had Richard Corbet, the episcopal Merrythought, come to his see in 1629 (no less than eighty-eight years since the original grant) than he again reopened the whole matter. Vehement litigation followed, and we hear the last of the matter in a plaintive letter, dated June 1, 1629, in the State Papers. It is addressed to Secretary Dorchester by Corbet. He thinks a recent

"suit of his was unsuccessful, on account of the way in which it was commenced. He is confident of success through the Secretary, because it is conceived he has done some tolerable service to his Majesty lately. His lawyers advise him to try his cause in one of their courts; but if he ever tries more courts than that he is in, let a lawyer be his poison. If Gloucester Hall were in his possession, as it is injuriously kept from him, there were no question but he might challenge his immunity by Act of Parliament. When he was consecrated, he took an oath to be very hospitable; if these payments are put upon him, he must either be forsworn or undone."

It is indeed comforting to know that the Bishop was not reduced to any such perjury by the loss of the Hall; for Wood tells us how, when Bishop, he "would take the key of the wine-cellar, and he and his chaplain would go and lock themselves in and be merry."

The contention as to this Naboth's vineyard was finally set at rest by the action of his successor, John Bancroft, in building Cuddesdon Palace as an episcopal residence.

As soon as Sir Thomas White had carried out the necessary repairs, he leased the Hall to William Stocke, a Fellow of St. John's College, for a term of twenty years. On St. John the Baptist's Day, 1560, the first Principal and a hundred scholars took their commons in the old monks' refectory of Gloucester Hall. The first Principal was an old Fellow of Brasenose, from whence, "for his great proficiency in learning, he was taken by Sir Thomas White," and made one of the first Fellows of St. John's. One event only marked his first principality. In September of this year Amy Robsart, whose sudden death and obscure burial at Cumnor had excited general suspicion, was taken up by order of Robert Dudley, Earl of Leicester, that she might be reburied in St. Mary's Church. She was

"secretly brought by night to Gloucester College without the town of Oxford, the which place was hanged with blake cloth, and garnished with skocheons of his armes and hers in pale—that is to say, a great chamber where the mourners did dine, and that where the gentlewomen did dine, and benethe the stairs a great hall, all which places, as aforesaid, were hanged with blake cloth, and garnished with scutcheons: the which being thus furnished, there the corse lay till the burial, and till such time as all things were ready for the same."

Hence she was moved to St. Mary's, where Dr. Babington, "my lord's Chaplaine," making the public funeral sermon at her second burial, "tript once or twice in his speech by recommending to their memories that vertuous ladie so pittefully murdered, instead of so pitifully slain."

In 1563 William Stocke left Gloucester Hall to

become President of St. John's, and he assigned his lease, or sublet, to William Palmer, an old member of Brasenose, who lived to suffer much for the Catholic religion which he professed. But after little more than a year William Stocke came back, having resigned the Presidency of St. John's from a whimsical fear of being deprived, and he remained Principal till 1573, a period during which the Hall flourished greatly. In 1574 he left of his own accord, and "after conferring upon him of several benefices, if not a dignity or two, which he changed for others, such was the rambling of his mind, died, notwithstanding, in a mean condition, yet always *in animo Catholicus*, in 1607."

In his time arose a practice of letting apartments in the College to various tenants. The lodgers were mostly men of good position. A list of members of the Hall in 1572 includes twenty-two persons who were not ordinary undergraduates, nor yet ordinary tutors. Of these no less than fourteen were knights, and one an Archdeacon. One of the most distinguished was probably Sir George Peckham, who gave £100 for the repair of the College in 1573. He occupied the Principal's lodgings; for when William Stocke retired from the College in 1573, it was arranged that it might be covenanted that Sir George Peckham might quietly enjoy his lodging there. He was a merchant adventurer, who petitioned the Queen "to allow of an enterprise by them conceived at their charges and adventure to be performed for England, and for the honour of her Majesty." The result was the foundation of a colony in Newfoundland. It is obvious indeed, from the number of people who died there, that the inhabitants of

CATHOLICS AT GLOUCESTER HALL

Gloucester Hall consisted of a different class to that which generally inhabited a college. In 1577 and 1578 alone there were three deaths of members of the Hall, who were buried in the church of St. Thomas. In 1600 we find John Feteplace occupying the Principal's lodgings, for Anthony Bushop, one of the serjeants of Abingdon, died in his house on February 11 of that year. In 1609 Richard Gatagre, M.A., Fellow of All Souls in 1550, and Esquire Bedell of Arts, died in the Hall, aged eighty-eight. Thomas Miller, Fellow of New College, died in the Hall in 1643. These are only a few out of a large number of similar entries.

There were women as well as men in the Hall. The first recorded lady was Lady Catesby, who was here in 1577. Two widows died in the College in 1616—Mrs. Joan Ingram, widow of Mr. Richard Ingram, and Mrs. Anne Coles. Mrs. Susanna Holland, widow of Dr. Thomas Holland, sometime Regius Professor of Divinity, died here on March 4, 1650. And for one of whom we hear in this way there must have been many more of whom we hear nothing.

But a far more interesting, if more obscure, class of tenants were the Roman Catholics, open or concealed. First must be mentioned three Fellows of Trinity—George Blackwell, who was residing in the College in 1572; Thomas Allen, who arrived almost at the same date, and took up his quarters for a sixty-years' residence on No. 9 staircase; and, thirdly, Thomas Warren, who went to Gloucester Hall in 1579.

These facts hardly served to give Gloucester Hall a good reputation. In later days it was always referred to as a hotbed of Popery.

"Fanaticks keep their children at home, or breed them in private schools under fanaticks, or send them beyond seas, though before the war they did not, but did send them to the University to Gloucester College."

The first three Principals of the Hall, at any rate, were all Catholics *in animo*, if not in profession; and at one or very nearly the same time—namely, between 1570 and 1580—we find a dozen or so of the most prominent Catholics in England among the residents in Gloucester Hall. Scarcely less distinguished than Thomas Allen was Edmund Rainolds, a Catholic, who lived for sixty years next door to Allen on No. 8 staircase. But these were passive, and not active, Catholics. The same cannot be said of George Blackwell, who went straight from Gloucester Hall to Douai. He was one of the priests who carried on active missionary work in England. He lived for three days in the Countess of Arundel's secret chamber, where he was in danger of being starved. In 1597 he was appointed Archpriest by Clement VIII., and his subsequent history with the dissensions he caused in the Catholic party are well known. Not less famous is Dr. William Bishop, who was at Gloucester Hall probably in 1572. He was a bitter opponent of Blackwell, and suffered imprisonment both from Walsingham and Cajetan. In 1622, chiefly by his exertions, the office of Archpriest was abolished, and he became the first missionary Bishop in England, under the title of Bishop of Chalcedon. An even more interesting figure is Sir William Catesby, a Catholic gentleman belonging to a most ill-fated family. He and his wife were resident in the College in 1577. Here a daughter was born to Lady Catesby in the lodgings that Sir George Peckham repaired.

"She did pay her chrysom, and all other duties, to the Vicar and clark of St. Thomas's parish. The said child was not christened by the said Vicar, but by a Popish priest."

Sir William Catesby was deeply compromised as a Catholic. He was a subscriber to the College at Douai, and he was fined for not attending at church. Two of his sons, better known than himself, were members of Gloucester Hall. Ralph Sheldon and Henry Lawson were two other members of the Hall, who came of families that were noted for their devotion to the Catholic cause. The family of Lawson, in particular, has sent more recruits to the Jesuit order than any other in England.

It is no wonder that so ominous a conjunction attracted the notice of the authorities. There are two amusing entries in the State Papers which point to the suspicion under which the Hall laboured. The first is a presentment, dated November 15, 1577, in the College of Gloucester, of "William Meredith, suspected to be an Horrible Papist, and esteemed to be worth £50." The second is fourteen years later, dated April 20, 1591:

"John Allyn, of Gloucester Hall, Oxford, said Mass on Good Friday, and made the blood of Christ sent from Rome drop 9 or 10 drops of fresh bloode, for which £20 a drop is given, and it may not be touched till given by a priest: those who have it about them can sustain no danger of body. They have private prayers for the Earl of Arundel's preservation."

At the same time, if English authorities feared as to the state of Gloucester Hall, the many representatives of the old faith who were now abroad had their hopes. This is strikingly exemplified by a legacy contained in the will of Richard Pate, Bishop of Worcester (1541). He had been a prisoner in the Tower from 1560 to 1563, and he died at Louvain on November 23 or October 5, 1565. Mass is still said for his soul in the English College at Rome annually on the latter date. His will is dated from the Tower of London, February 12, 1561:

"I do bequeath the revenues of my two annuities, the one in Monte della fede and the other in Monte della farina within Rome, unto the Right Reverend Father in God Thomas Goldwell, my Lord Assaphen, and my dear friend Mr. Henry Pinyngses, to such uses as I have declared in writing. The annuities to be conveyed to the Cathedral Church of Worcester. During the time of this schism goes in the realm no one penny of the said annuity, nor any knowledge thereof should come unto the mentioned Cathedral Church. When it shall please God to send the return of our realm to the unity of Christe's Church, then I would have you convey the instrument before made by you of any donation thereof unto my Cathedral Church, and then the said annuities to be employed on *inter alia* xx marks to be given in exhibycion to the help and furtherance of iiii scholars and students in Gloucester College in the University of Oxford, and that Worcestershire men to have the preference thereof, and for lack of them Oxfordshire men to be preferred."

This local preference attaching to Worcestershire is peculiarly interesting, when one bears in mind the later history of the Hall.

As a mere matter of conjecture, one may throw out a suggestion that the strange story of Nicholas Wadham's College at Venice may have arisen from a garbled and confused recollection of several facts. There was, first, Nicholas Wadham's avowed intention to plant his College in Gloucester Hall; secondly, the pronounced Roman Catholic bent of Gloucester Hall at this date; and, thirdly, the remarkable bequest which was then waiting, and presumably still is waiting, for Gloucester Hall in Italy. And we can well understand how a confused tradition might arise that Nicholas Wadham intended to found a College for English Roman Catholics at Venice.

But though the leaders of thought and the seniority of Gloucester Hall were Catholic in their aspirations, we do not think there is any reason to believe that this was true of the ordinary body of students. It is more likely that a successful educational establishment was used to mask the true character of the place. Of some of the students we can say definitely that not only were they not Papists, but that they were active supporters of the Reformation. Among these was Philip Stubbs, who, "having a restless and hot head," settled at Gloucester Hall, where his brother or near kinsman, Justinian Stubbs, occurs in 1589. He was a most rigid Calvinist, a bitter enemy to Popery, and a great corrector of the vices of his time—witness his "Anatomie of Abuses." It is remarkable, too, that the three members of the Jesuit order whom we have been able to trace as members of Gloucester Hall were all members of the Reformed Church while at Oxford. These were John Falkner, *alias* Dingley, who was converted by Lord Windsor during the Essex expedition to Spain—he was chaplain during the siege of Windsor Castle, and died in England at the age of eighty-two; Francis Geoffry, *alias* John Fowler, a man of a good Catholic family, who actually lapsed into heresy at Oxford under the education of Master Case; and Henry Stanton, *alias* Anthony Cantlett, who was a "schismatic" till his seventeenth year.

Of Henry Russell, Principal of Gloucester Hall (1572 to 1579), in succession to William Stocke, we know little more than the name. William Stocke's twenty-years' lease had not yet expired, and Russell was probably his deputy rather than active Principal. It is even doubtful whether he became Principal as early as 1572, since some manuscript letters of this date say he was elected on January 15, 1576. Worcester College and its predecessors appear to have been constantly involved in litigation, and Henry Russell was no exception. He was fined £100 by the Court of Star Chamber for ejecting a certain widow Sawyer from a farm belonging to St. John's College, and subletting it to the above-named Justinian Stubbs. His successor, Christopher Bagshaw, occupies a more prominent position in the history of England. He came of a Derbyshire family, and graduated at Balliol in 1572. He was a Fellow of Balliol with Parsons, the Jesuit, who became his lifelong enemy. At this time he was zealous in his devotion to Protestant principles, " yet proved troublesome in his public disputes, and his behaviour towards persons." He was the first Principal of Gloucester Hall who was not a Fellow of St. John's, and was the nominee of Robert Dudley, Earl of Leicester, the Chancellor of the University. After two years he resigned the Principality, retired into France, and was converted to Romanism. Henceforth he was a stormy petrel in the

Catholic party. At Paris he was known as the "Doctor Erraticus." Going to Rome, he was expelled from the English College, and at length, while on a mission to England in 1587, found lodgings in the Tower. In 1593 he was among the miscellaneous prisoners of Wisbech Gaol, and was pronounced by Father Edmonds to be a man of "no worth, unruly, disordered, and a disobedient person, not to be favoured or respected by any." He was the reputed author of "The True Relation of the Faction begun at Wisbech." He ended his days on the Continent, and died at Paris after 1625, when he cannot have been far short of eighty. Of John Delabere we can say little but that the Hall flourished exceedingly in his day. In the first year of his office he brought no less than thirty-seven members of the Hall to matriculate, a number that has probably never been exceeded in the history of the Hall or College. He was, like several of his successors, a Doctor of Physic (of the University of Basil). He was originally a member of Christchurch, and of his history after his resignation of the Hall we know nothing, save the rather vague fact vouchsafed by Wood—"that he was living in the marches of Wales, near Ludlow, in 1616." Hitherto the Hall had flourished—in point of numbers, at any rate. Under John Hawley, Doctor of Laws, and late Fellow of St. John's, it declined in this respect. From 1595 to 1600 the matriculations were very few. Then followed three good years, and after that, for the rest of the Principality of John Hawley, there were seldom more than three or four matriculations a year. It was during this period that the Hall so narrowly escaped becoming Wadham College. Nicholas Wadham had fixed upon it as the site of his College, and Dorothy Wadham sought to carry out his intention and purchase it. But the Principal, Dr. Hawley, refused to resign his interest in the Hall unless the foundress named him the first Warden. There were difficulties, too, in the way of St. John's College parting with the property. Certainly our fate in this respect has been unique. We escaped from being St. John's by a dream, and from becoming Wadham by a Principal; we have been a refuge for the Irishry, and a shelter for the Scotch when Balliol looked askance at them; we were selected by Aubrey to be "his school and University in one"; and we actually became a College for the Greek nation. With fates so various constantly threatening us, we were only saved by the hazardous operation of a Chancery action from continuing to be Gloucester Hall, while our endowments were dedicated to the foundation of a College on the site of Magdalen Hall.

The only other incident of John Hawley's reign that can be placed on record is an attempt to rebuild or restore the chapel, and for this purpose St. John's College made a grant of six timber trees out of Bagley Wood in 1608. John Hawley died at Gloucester Hall, in 1626, at the age of sixty, and was buried at Kertlington on April 2 in that year.

CHAPTER VI

1626—1692

DEGORY WHEARE—THE CIVIL WAR AND THE RESTORATION—BYROM EATON—THE MEMBERS OF GLOUCESTER HALL

THE history of a hall is to a far greater extent than that of a college the history of its Principal, and the advent of Degory Wheare marks a new era in the history of Gloucester Hall.

A Cornishman by birth—born at Berry Court, Jacobstow, in Cornwall, in 1573—he had matriculated at Broadgates Hall on July 6, 1593. In 1597 he took the degree of B.A., and he became M.A. in 1600. After spending some time as tutor of the Hall, he was elected to a Cornish Fellowship at Exeter in 1602, and to an ordinary Fellowship in 1603. While at Broadgates Hall he had been a tutor of John Pym, and in later years, when he became Principal of Gloucester Hall, John Pym sent his son Alexander to be educated under his old tutor, and himself contributed to the restoration of the Hall.

In 1608 Wheare resigned his Fellowship at Exeter in

order to become travelling companion to Grey Brydges, "the King of the Cotswolds," afterwards fifth Lord Chandos, during a prolonged tour in Europe. On his return to England he remained in the service of Lord Chandos, and the connection was only broken by the death of his patron, on August 10, 1621. Chandos had been a friend of Thomas Allen, and it was doubtless this fact that now brought Degory Wheare and his wife to take up their lodgings in Gloucester Hall on the death of his patron. At first he occupied no official position, but was simply a tenant of John Hawley, the Principal. Soon afterwards, however, he attained a post which gave him dignity in the University, and brought credit on the Hall to which he had attached himself.

In 1621 it became known that William Camden was about to establish and endow a lecture in history, now known as the Camden Professorship of Ancient History. On November 19, 1621, Thomas Allen wrote to Camden, recommending Wheare for the post as a man who, " besides his abilities of learning sufficient for such a place, is known to be of good experience, and having sometime travelled, and of very honest and discreet conversation." There was another candidate in the field in the person of Daniel Gardiner, a Fellow of New College, a man of remarkable attainments, if we are to believe his testimonial, which stated that he "remembered everything which had been done anywhere." However, the influence of Thomas Allen was sufficient to secure the place for Wheare.

Of Wheare's personal qualities we know little. Wood says that he was esteemed "by some a learned and genteel man, by others a Calvinist." That he enjoyed a considerable reputation in the University is undoubted. He published his lectures in book form, and entitled them "De Ratione et Methodo Legendi Historias," a title which was altered in the third edition into "Relectiones Hyemales de Ratione et Methodo Legendi Historias." The book ran through many editions, and was a well-known text-book, even in the eighteenth century. Perhaps his letters to Camden afford the best information as to his character. They are fulsome in the extreme, even beyond the habit of the age. One of them, dated March 12, 1622, is a splendid example of the begging letter of the period. He tells how he has been reduced to poverty by the "profligacy and laziness of a certain cook," and suggests that, unless the laws assist him, he will be indebted to Camden for all that he and his "numerosa proles" eat or drink or wear.

After Camden's death, he celebrated his memory from the chair founded by him in a discourse which, with a collection of laudatory verses by Brian Twyne, R. Burton, and other Oxford notabilities, appeared under the title of "Camdeni Insignia." On the whole, we seem to observe in him a considerable resemblance to his perhaps more illustrious successor, Benjamin Woodroffe. Each of them was energetic and learned, each of them did great service to the Hall, but each was afflicted by chronic domestic troubles, which detracted somewhat from their dignity, and were apt to give them the air of adventurers among the weightier members of Oxford society.

That Degory Wheare was at first a good Principal

there can be no doubt. From the date of his arrival in College the numbers of the matriculations increased rapidly. From 1600 to 1621 the average number of matriculations had been less than five per annum, and in the last five years of that period they had generally been only two or three; but after Wheare's arrival in 1621 there were eleven, in 1622 there were nine, in 1623 there were eight, and after he became Principal in 1629 there were eleven, in 1630 there were fourteen, in 1632 there were nineteen, and the high-water mark was reached in 1634, when there were twenty-three.

John Hawley was buried on April 2, 1626. On the fourth of the same month Degory Wheare was admitted to succeed him, a fact which shows that he had for some time been regarded as his natural successor. His first task in his new office was to restore the buildings, which must have been in a sad state of dilapidation. A manuscript written on vellum in the College library, one of the few memorials the College possesses of its Gloucester Hall days, records the progress of the scheme. The volume was commenced in 1630. Its Latin preface calls to mind some of the letters relating to that early chapel of Gloucester College, which had now fallen into ruins. It speaks of the chapel like the original chapel *jamdudum inchoatum*. It had been projected as long ago as 1608. The Principal and students, "trusting in Divine assistance," had finished it, and they were anxious to immortalize the memory of those who had contributed towards the completion of the work. The record of donations to the Hall was carefully kept up to 1640. But here there is a lacuna. No doubt Wheare's energies were failing him, and there are at this date other signs that he was unequal to the government of the Hall.

The record is taken up again by Tobias Garbrand in 1653, with a reference to the Civil Wars, which had treated " the halls in so uncivil a manner." He expressed his intention of carrying on the Hall in the same way as previously, as far as that was possible; but he was not able to continue the spirit of the founder of the book. His handwriting, rough and illegible, the handwriting which as a doctor he had doubtless used, according to immemorial tradition, in the penning of prescriptions, affords a striking contrast to the beautiful and careful penmanship of Degory Wheare. Very soon the book drops altogether, and there is no further entry till 1695.

Benjamin Woodroffe, energetic in this as in most things, takes up the pen in the severe classical handwriting which has survived almost to the present day to record two gifts of peculiar interest, no less than the gift of Vol. I. of the Philosophical Transactions, and "Heydon's Astrological Discourses," by John Aubrey, to the library. There were two more entries, and then a half-finished entry, and the record ends. Doubtless Dr. Woodroffe was too busy with his Greek students to pay any more attention to it.

The subscriptions collected in this way for the chapel in 1630 amounted to £96 10s. There were certain regular payments made by members of the College, and certain payments made by strangers. A Master of Arts on being admitted invariably paid £3 to the fund, and a Bachelor of Arts £1, on taking this degree. A member of the Hall who was admitted *inter com-*

mensales superioris ordinis, a standing which probably corresponded to that of the gentleman commoner of later days, paid £2 10s. or £3. The list includes several celebrated names. John Pym gives 20s., and his son, an old member of the Hall, a like sum; Thomas Clayton, Regius Professor of Medicine, last Principal of Broadgates Hall, and first Master of Pembroke, gave £2. He was an old member and tutor of Gloucester Hall. Sir Kenelm Digby gave £2; John Rouse, Librarian of the Public Library, £1 2s.; Henry Briggs, Savilian Professor of Geometry and Fellow of Merton, gave 20s.; John Hales, known as the "walking library," Fellow of Merton and Eton, gave 20s.; William Burton, lately Greek Lecturer at the Hall, Master of the Grammar School at Kingston-on-Thames, and celebrated by Wood as "an excellent Latinist, noted philologist, well skilled in the tongues, an excellent critic and antiquary, and therefore beloved of all learned men of his time, especially of the famous Usher, Archbishop of Armagh," gave £2 10s.; Samuel Fell, Dean of Christchurch, gave £5; and the veteran tutor, Edmund Rainolds, gave a like sum; William Gilbert, "a general scholar and a rare man," member of the Hall, and M.P. for Dublin University (1639-1654), gave 20s.; "Waterworks" Sandys gave £2 4s.; Jonathan Browne, afterwards Dean of Hereford and Canon of Westminster, gave £10 in all. Lastly, Roger Griffin, citizen of Oxford and member of the College of Pistores, gave 2,000 *scandularia,* worth 22s., and Richard Cluett, Archdeacon of Middlesex, gave 20s.

Of this sum, £88 was spent on the chapel, and the vouchers for the payments " can be seen in the Principal's hands." The items were as follows :—

"Imprimis fabro murario sive caementario, 25*li.* 10*s.* Materiario sive fabro tignario, 38*li.* 10*s.* Gypsatori et scandulario, 10*li.* 11*s.* Vitriario, 4*li.* 6*s.* Fabro ferrario, 7*li.* 10*s.* Pictori, 1*li.* 4*s.* Storealatori, 9*s.*"

Books were purchased with the balance—a Latin Bible, Seneca, Cicero and Livy, a volume of Copernicus, and others. In 1632 sums were raised for the restoration of the Hall. Among others, Clement Barksdale gave £3 on taking his Master's degree; £18 were received, and £22 expended. Thomas Allen's legacy of £10 was devoted to the payment of the balance. A bookcase, *parieti inferiori sacelli affixum,* and the "Universal History of Thuanus," were purchased with the remainder. There was another considerable present of books in this year.

In 1634 John Sambatch gave a silver cup inscribed with his name, and a copy of Thomas Aquinas. Another silver cup was purchased out of two donations of £3. Euclid, Tacitus, Paterculus, and other volumes were purchased out of a present from the family of Whorwood, of Holton, a member of which matriculated at the Hall. Donations were very numerous in the next three years, and consisted almost entirely of books, though several pieces of plate were purchased, and some old silver which had become worn out was melted down and remade. In 1638 the money received was spent on the repair of the Hall by the "obsonator," and in the following year on the repair of the "promptuarium" and other works. Among other subscribers were Christopher Merritt and John Wheare, a son of the Principal, one of the above-named *numerosa proles.* An interesting entry is that of a subscription of 40s. towards the expenses of entertaining the King and Queen in 1636.

Two papers signed by Degory Wheare, and dated 1631, now in the Archives of the University, throw some light on the customs and expenses of the Hall. Commoners paid on admission 4s. to the house and 4s. to the College officers, the manciple, butler and cook; semi-commoners or battlers paid 2s. to the house, and 1s. 6d. to the officers; a poor scholar paid nothing. Every commoner paid a penny a week to the butler, and a halfpenny to the servitors of the Hall. He paid 1s. a quarter for wages to the manciple and cook, and besides this a varying sum for decrements, a term which covered kitchen fuel, tablecloths, utensils and the like. This item sometimes amounted to 5s. a quarter, but never more. On taking any degree, 10s. was paid to the Principal, and another 10s. to the house, or else there was given a presentation dinner. The Principal received the rent of the chambers, which he kept in repair, and paid quarterly to two moderators or readers the sum of £1 6s. 8d. It appears that it was the custom for every commoner to take his turn as steward, go to market with the manciple and cook, see the provisions bought for ready money, apportion the amount for each meal, oversee the divisions at dinner and supper, and be accountable for any commons sent to private chambers. At the end of every quarter the accounts were inspected by the Principal and such of the masters as he pleased to send for. On Act Monday it had been customary for the proceeding masters to keep a common supper in the Hall, but this charge had of late years been devoted to the building of an oratory, the flooring of the hall, and the purchase of plate and of books. The manciple received eightpence a week from the community, and eightpence a quarter from every commoner; also poundage from the baker, brewer, butterman, cheeseman and mercer, etc. The butler had eightpence a day from the community, and a penny a week from each commoner, also daily the chippings of bread and the waste beer. The cook had like payments, besides " the offals of the kitchen."

The palmy days of the Hall under Degory Wheare when there were " a hundred students in the hall and some being persons of quality ten or twelve went in their doublets of cloth of silver and gold," ended about 1640. In that year, and in every succeeding year of his Principality, the matriculations fell off, and it is plain that there was some circumstance adverse to the Hall which retarded its prosperity. It may be that Wheare, who was now sixty-seven, was incapacitated from doing his work. There is a letter from Wheare to Archbishop Laud, dated January 21, 1640, which points to the fact without explaining the cause:

" I am infinitely obliged to you in respect of that favour you did me by Mr. President for the settling of all differences which may and are likely to arise between St. John's College and myself touching the place I hold in Gloucester Hall. I am now content upon the conditions proposed to resign my interest, but because I cannot suddenly resolve upon whom your favour should devolve, my son being out of town, I pray two or three weeks' grace for the better settling of it for my future content."

This letter points to an immediate resignation of the Principality. We can only conjecture that the conditions proposed were that his son should succeed him, and that the negotiations fell through when this proposal was not accepted.

Already people in the University were looking about for probable successors to him in his various posts, and there is a very amusing letter complaining that the reversion of the history lecture, to which the writer considered himself entitled, was lost through the obstinate longevity of the Principal. "The place which is settled on Mr. Wheare, now almost of the age of eighty, is not like for the present to be void."

Meanwhile the Hall itself was falling on evil days. There were hardly any members in residence, and by a warrant under the Privy Seal to the Exchequer, "Legg caused to be erected a mill for grinding swords at Woolvercott, county Gloucester, and forges at Gloucester Hall." This was in 1644. On August 1, 1647, Degory Wheare died, at the age of seventy-four, and was buried on the 3rd under the great eagle in Exeter College Chapel.

His son Charles was the most successful of his children. He was in 1645 the first Gloucester Hall Proctor. Wood notes in this year that "In defect of a statutable master of Corpus, whose turn it was to elect, the election fell to the halls, who elected Charles Wheare." Other sons of Degory Wheare were: Degory, who died in 1627; John, who died in 1642; Samuel, who was Vicar of Lanncells, in Cornwall, in 1661; and William, who was Fellow of Merton, and died in 1634. Of these five sons, only two appear to have survived him. Of the rest of his children Wood rather spitefully says: "He left behind him a widow and children, who soon after became poor; and whether the Females lived honestly 'tis not for me to dispute it." Charles Wheare did his best to secure the Camden Lecture in place of his father, and it is said he had been specially trained for the post; but the change of government and other circumstances lost him the reversion.

John Maplett of Christchurch was nominated to succeed Wheare by the Marquis of Hertford. He was a son of John Maplett, "a sufficient shoemaker" of St. Martin's-le-Grand. Like a later principal, Dr. Woodroffe, he was a scholar of Westminster, who was elected to Christchurch in 1630, at the age of eighteen. He became B.A. in 1634, M.A. in 1636, Proctor in 1643, and M.D. in 1647. He was almost immediately ejected by the visitors, though he does not appear to have been by any means a violent politician. He left Gloucester Hall and became tutor to the young Lord Falkland. He submitted to the visitors of Christchurch in 1651, and is then represented as being on leave of absence.

His successor, Tobias Garbrand, belonged to a well-known family. Herks Garbrand was a Dutch bookseller, who fled from persecution in Holland, and established himself as a bookseller and wine merchant in Oxford in or about 1546. His sons and grandsons were well known in Oxford. Some carried on the bookselling business, and others entered Oxford colleges, two at least becoming Fellows of Magdalen. The grandson of the original Herks Garbrand was Vice-President of Magdalen, and died at the age of fifty-nine, and it was probably his son who was now appointed Principal of Gloucester Hall. He was one of the delegates to the

Parliamentary visitors who were appointed on September 30, 1647, but this is all we hear of him in connection with the visitation. His duties can scarcely have been onerous, as during the greater part of his term of office there were no undergraduates in the Hall. When the Restoration came he quietly retreated into the country. Like his predecessor and successor, Dr. Maplett, he was a doctor by profession, "a dissenting physician," as Wood calls him. He retired to Abingdon, and practised his faculty there. He died on April 7, 1689, at the age of eighty or more, and is buried in the church of St. Helens in that town. He had at least two children—Tobias Garbrand, a barrister and writer of several books, who lost his practice by an attempt to prove that the Duke of York was not a Catholic; and a daughter, who married Thomas Dawson, a noted Nonconformist preacher and writer.

With the Restoration, John Maplett returned from Bath to take charge of at least five undergraduates. On December 19, 1660, they celebrated the Restoration in proper style. Under this date Wood has an entry: "A play acted at Glocester Hall, cald 'The Ordinary,' out of spite." The play was doubtless that of William Cartwright, written in 1643, and bearing this title. It is in Hazlitt's "Collection of Plays." Gloucester Hall has always been a favourite place for plays, and Wood speaks of plays acted by stealth "in Kettle Hall, or at Holywell Mill, or in the refectory at Gloucester Hall." John Maplett, however, soon found his position either too laborious or too expensive. He returned to Bath in 1662, and died on August 4, 1670, aged fifty-five. He was "learned, candid and ingenious,

DECLINE OF GLOUCESTER HALL

good physician, a better Christian, and an excellent Latin," says Wood. Withal he " was of a tender, brittle constitution, inclining to feminine, clear-skinned, and of a very fresh complexion." He was one of the first physicians to go to Bath, and he wrote a Latin treatise on the beneficial effects of Bath waters, which was published by Guidott after his death. Guidott also erected a black marble tablet to his memory in the north aisle of Bath Abbey.

His successor was Byrom Eaton, who was Principal for nearly thirty years, during which it is almost impossible to discover anything he did in connection with the Hall.

For the first twelve years of his reign the Hall seems to have been in a fairly flourishing condition. In 1663 there were six, in 1664 five, in 1666 seven, in 1667 twelve, in 1668 twelve, in 1669 fourteen matriculations.

Byrom Eaton was born in 1613, and matriculated at Brasenose on February 21, 1634. He became B.A. 1635, M.A. 1641. In this year he was elected Fellow of his College, and in 1646 he was Junior Proctor, and subsequently Senior Proctor on the death of Richard Wyatt. In 1648 his College was visited by the Parliamentary visitors, and he expressed himself willing "with all humble reverence to submit to any authority not derogatory to the knowne laws of the land, the statutes and privileges of the University and my College, and my several legal oaths and obligations." He was expelled from the University for non-submission five days later, but he remained in Oxford till June 29, when the soldiers were ordered to drive him out, if necessary. By some means, however, he made his peace with the visitors, and was reinstated in his Fellowship in October on condition that he leave his living before Easter. He took the degree of D.D. at the Restoration, and became Rector of Nuneham Courtenay in the same year. He was appointed Archdeacon of Stow by Dr. Barlow in 1677, and Archdeacon of Leicester in 1683.

The Hall soon fell into a state of hopeless disrepair.

"In 1675, 1676, 1677, 1678 not one scholar" (says Wood) "in Gloucester Hall, onlie the principall and his family and two or three more families that live there in some part to keep it from ruin. The paths are grown over with grass, the way into the hall and chappel made up with boards."

Prideaux tells the same tale in 1676. Writing on September 18, he says:

"Gloucester Hall is like to be demolished, the charge of chimney money being so great that Byrom Eaton will scarce live there any longer. There hath been no scholars there these three or four years: for all which time the hall being in arrears for this tax the collectors have at last fallen upon the principal, who being by the act liable to the payment hath made great complaints about the town and created us very good sport: but the old fool hath been forced to pay the money, which hath amounted to a considerable sum."

The desolation of the Hall left it an easy prey to robbers, and the second recorded burglary took place on October 20, 1687,

"between the hours of 12 and 1 in the night time when twelve men armed entered Gloucestre Hall at the great gate, being let in as is supposed by one that got in before

SOUTHERN BUILDINGS, FROM THE GARDEN

From a photograph by the [*Oxford Camera Club*]

the gate was shut, got a great leaver or piece of timber, wrenched open the barrs of a lower window: entered all with lighted candells, went to their beds' sides and awak'd them, bound their hands and feet except Dr. Eaton's: took away 6 or 7 pieces of plate belonging to the hall, all Dr. Eaton's plate, his porringer, silver spoones, trencher plates, rings, jewells, silk petticotes and waiscots belonging to his daughters, other clothes: which done they went down into the lower room, eat up what they could find, drink his drink (3 or 4 bottles of wine), drank 'the young ladies' healths': tarried till near 4 and so departed. His losses about 300*li*."

Wood adds the only piece of information we have about his personal character:

"This man hath lost severall sons, and none but daughters left: hath been rob'd twice in 2 or 3 yeares: yet he is sordid still, and nothing will change his base humour."

It must have been soon after this melancholy episode that Byrom Eaton resolved to retire from the Hall. From 1683 to 1692 there was only one matriculation at the Hall, though two persons took their B.A. degree in 1692.

On May 19 of that year Dr. Byrom Eaton resigned. The longevity of members of Gloucester Hall is truly remarkable, in an age when life was much shorter than it is at present. William Stocke attained the age of seventy-nine; Thomas Allen and Edmund Rainolds were nonagenarians; Richard Gatagre lived to eighty-eight, and Christopher Bagshaw to eighty; Tobias Garbrand must have been very nearly the same age when he died; Wheare attained seventy-four; John Delabere must have been seventy-six when he was "living in the marches of Wales"; Benjamin Woodroffe died at the age of seventy-three; and Byrom Eaton survived his resignation eleven years, and died at the age of ninety, in November, 1703. If only he had continued to live at Gloucester Hall, it is probable that he would have survived the Hall itself. He was buried at Nuneham Courtenay. A portrait of him presented by his housekeeper, Mrs. Mary Moulden, hangs in the College. The same lady presented a portrait of his daughter, Sarah Eaton, in November, 1739, the lady whose noble benefaction to the College still keeps his memory green.

Two abortive schemes in connection with the Hall deserve notice in this place. The first was the benefaction of John Warner, Bishop of Rochester, who died in 1666. He bequeathed £80 a year, to issue out of his Manor of Swayton, in Lincolnshire, for the maintenance of four scholars of the Scottish nation at Balliol College, to be chosen from time to time by the Archbishop of Canterbury and Bishop of Rochester, each to have £20 yearly till they were masters. The gift was made in 1666, at which time the donor died; but "the overseers for the time being not willing to place the said scholars in this College, neither the masters nor the fellows altogether willing to receive them, as not being in any way advantageous to the house, thoughts were had of making Gloucester Hall a College for them, and some of them were thereupon placed there. At length, when Dr. Good became Master of the College in 1672, he took order that they should be translated to Balliol, and there they yet continue." But the change did not take place before Scotland had given Gloucester Hall at least one distinguished member in the person of Michael Geddes, noted as an anti-Catholic writer, who became English Chaplain at Lisbon, and fell under the ban of the Inquisition in that city.

The second was a fantastic scheme of John Aubrey, connected with the Great Horse controversy. We get merely a passing mention of it, but it should be noted as perhaps the most fantastic of the many plans for the rehabilitation of Gloucester Hall. It occurs in the "Idea of the Education of Young Gentlemen," a treatise which was completed in 1694, but never published. It involved the erection of six or seven schools, each of which should be both school and university, in different parts of England. "Gloucester Hall in Oxford would be a good place for one of these schools, but it would be envied by the colleges."

As this chapter practically ends the history of the Hall as such, it may be well to speak of the great men who at one time or another passed to and fro within its gates. A few names stand out prominently, and are still in the mouths of men; others there were who were great in their day, but now are only remembered by those who love to dig among the dust.

In the first class are Richard Lovelace, Carew the regicide, Thomas Coryate, Robert Catesby, and Kenelm Digby, a not undistinguished collection for a Hall that was always small in numbers. The academic career of Richard Lovelace is one of peculiar interest.

"He became" (says Wood) "a gentleman commoner of Gloucester Hall in the beginning of the year 1634, and in that of his age 16, being then accounted the most amiable and beautiful person that ever eye beheld—a person also of innate modesty, virtue and courtly deportment which made him then much admired and adored by the female sex. In 1636, when the king and queen were for some days entertained at Oxford, he was at the request of a great lady belonging to the queen actually created among other persons of quality Master of Arts, though but of two years standing: at which time his conversation being made public and consequently his ingenuity and generous soul discovered, he became as much admired by the male as before by the female sex."

No less picturesque was Kenelm Digby, whose career it is unnecessary for us to attempt to describe. " He was such a goodly, handsome person, gigantique and great voice, and had so graceful elocution and noble addresse, that had he been dropped out of the Clouds in any part of the world, he would have made himself respected." The learned Mr. Thomas Allen was wont to say that he was the Mirandula of the age. We pass to tragedy when we speak of Robert Catesby, who with his brother came to Gloucester Hall in 1586, and of John Carew, who was at Gloucester Hall in 1637. There is a resemblance between the fate of the two men, though their opinions were so widely different. Each was a wild enthusiast, a zealous supporter of a lost cause; each met his death bravely: Catesby at Ashby St. Ledgers, standing back to back with Percy, and fighting furiously, one bullet killing both conspirators; John Carew on the scaffold, though he had been offered many chances of escape, a Republican, without guile and without reproach. Lastly, we may mention in this class Thomas Coryate the Odcombian, who passed his life in wandering afoot a pauper pilgrim through the

East. The greatest of his exploits was the silencing of a laundry-woman, a famous scold, in her own Hindustani. The least of his books is now worth a greater sum than he probably ever carried in his pocket.

But we may leave these great names, and turn to those whose virtues or vices have not served to preserve their names. Foremost comes John Atherton, Bishop of Waterford, who suffered the penalty of death on a dreadful charge, proved, as some think, by the perjury of his adversaries. A more genial character is introduced to us by John Aubrey in the person of William Rumsey (1600). "He was an ingenious man and had a philosophical head. He was much troubled with phlegm, and being so one winter at the Court at Ludlow, where he was one of the counsellers, sitting by the fire spitting and spewling, he took a fine tender sprig and tied a rag at the end, and conceived he might put it down his throat and fetch up the plague, and he did so. Afterwards he made the instrument of whalebone." And John Aubrey pathetically adds, "I could never make it goe down my throat, but for those that can 'tis a most incomparable engine." Not only was this gentleman remarkable for his scientific attainments, but he had "so shrewd a head," that he was known as the picklock of the law. Another well-known Gloucester Hall lawyer was John Godolphin (1632), who was a Puritan Judge of the Admiralty Court in 1653. Our most noted academician, if we could claim him, was Ralph Bathurst (1634), who left Gloucester Hall for Trinity, where he became Fellow, and ultimately President and Vice-Chancellor, then Dean of Wells and Bishop of Bristol.

John Budden was one of the many scholars of note who were brought to Gloucester Hall by Thomas Allen. He became Regius Professor of Civil Law and Principal of Broadgates Hall. He was a "person of great eloquence, an excellent rhetorician, philosopher, and a most noted civilian." We have already referred to Thomas Clayton, who, like Budden, was a member of Gloucester Hall, a Regius Professor (of Medicine), Principal of Broadgates Hall, and Master of Pembroke. Edward Kelly, otherwise Talbot, had more adventures, but less reputation, than these learned professors. He, having an unsettled mind, left Oxford abruptly, and "in his rambles in Lancashire committing certain foul matters, lost his ears at Lancaster, and about that time caused by his incantations a poor man that had been buried in the yard belonging to Law Church, near to Walton-in-the-Dale, to be taken out of his grave, and to answer to such questions that he then proposed to him." Another equally unpleasant character was Philip Stubbs, who with his brother Justinian was "a most rigid Calvinist and a bitter enemy to poetry."

The Hall gave shelter to not a few distinguished foreigners, among others, to Camillus Cardoinus, a Neapolitan (1584); to John Drusius, who being admirably well read in the Hebrew, Chaldee and Syriac tongues, was recommended to the chief heads of the University (he afterwards migrated to Christchurch); to Francis Anthony Olevian (1616), a German of the Palatinate, who had studied ten years in the faculty of physic in the Universities of Heidelberg, Montpelier, Paris and Oxford; and to Anthony de Corro, Reader in

Divinity, though he was tainted, it is to be feared, with Pelagianism. As to Dermitius Meara, Wood registers a query, but adds that Gloucester Hall was a receptacle for Irishmen in his day. Most notable of all, however, was Theodore Haak, a German of the Palatinate, who, according to Weld, the historian of the Royal Society, gave the first occasion for and first suggested those informal meetings which resulted in the foundation of that society. Indeed, Gloucester Hall can claim several of the earliest Fellows. Sir Kenelm Digby forms the connecting-link between "King James, his academy of honour," and the society. Christopher Merritt, librarian of the Royal College of Physicians and friend of Harvey, was a member of the Council of the society at the date of its earliest published list. Ralph Bathurst and Benjamin Woodroffe, who was Fellow as early as 1668, are also included in the list.

Among men of science we must not forget Thomas Allen, who lived in the Hall for sixty years, and died there at the age of ninety-six. Queen Elizabeth sent for him "to have his advice about the new star that appeared in the Swan or Cassiopeia, to which he gave his judgment very learnedly." He was "honester than all the rest." The Earl of Leicester had so great respect for him, that he would several times have procured him a bishopric, but the desire of a sedate life and the good wishes he bore to the Church of Rome, would not suffer him to accept of it. "The vulgar did verily believe him to be a conjurer. He had a great many mathematical instruments and glasses in his chamber, which did also confirm the ignorant in their opinion; and his servitor, to impose on Freshmen and simple people, would tell them that sometimes he should meet the spirits coming up his stairs like bees." He was a legatee of Thomas Bodley—" My best gown and my best cloak I bequeath to Mr. William Gent of Gloucester Hall; and the next gown and cloak to my best I do bequeath to Mr. Thomas Allen of the same Hall." Fuller says of him that he succeeded to the skill and scandal of Friar Bacon, and he, with John Dee, was regarded by the vulgar as an atheist, and Leicester's agent for figuring and conjuring.

One of Thomas Allen's pupils was Sir John Davies, who wrote " many things in mathematics and astrology, but none of them extant." There went from hand to hand a volume of letters concerning chymical and magical secrets, which were written by this Sir John Davies, Dr. Dee, and Dr. Mat. Gwynne. He attained a greater prominence as chief of the ordnance of the Tower, and friend of the Earl of Essex. As such he was involved in Essex's treason, and sentenced to a traitor's death; but he was pardoned in 1601. The gossips said he earned his pardon by betraying his friends. He lived to send a son to Gloucester Hall, who bore the same name and title, but was not, as Wood is careful to inform us, the author of the " History of the Caribby Islands."

John Bainbridge, the first Savilian Professor of Astronomy in 1619, was another distinguished scientist, and William Cole, the physician, a great authority on epilepsy. In history, Sedgwick Harrison occupied the chair of Degory Wheare, while John Davies became Professor of Greek. Two turbulent divines deserve a passing notice—Richard Cox (1584) and Matthew

Griffith (1618). The latter spent many years of his life in Newgate.

Though there are many more names which are worthy of mention if space permitted, we must bring this catalogue of the alumni of Gloucester Hall to a close with a mere mention of the names of George Percy, one of the first Governors of Virginia, of John Grenville, Earl of Bath, and of Clement Barksdale, " the poet of the Cotswolds," who was for a great part of his life closely identified with the Hall.

CHAPTER VII

1692—1709

DR. WOODROFFE AND THE GREEK COLLEGE

On May 19, 1692, Dr. Byrom Eaton resigned his Principality of Gloucester Hall, and on August 15 following Dr. Benjamin Woodroffe was admitted Principal in his stead. The new Principal was a well-known character in Oxford. His father was one of the ejected clergy; he himself was born in Oxford in 1638, so that at the time of his appointment he was fifty-four. The distinguished position he held would at first sight lead us to suppose that he deserved a respect which he certainly did not inspire. Educated at Westminster, he was in turn student, Canon, sub-Dean, and Dean of Christchurch. The last office he held for only a few days. The appointment was made by James II., and cancelled by his successor in favour of Dean Aldrich. He was a fine scholar—a man of tireless energy and undaunted courage. He was familiar with Greek, French, Italian, Portuguese, and some of the Oriental languages—a very wide range of accomplishment for that day. He had been high in the favour of the Court, a chaplain of Charles II., and naval chaplain to James, Duke of York, at the time of the engagement with the Dutch at Southwold Bay in 1672. He was one of the earlier Fellows of the Royal Society, and that his fame was not merely local is shown by the fact that he was Lecturer of the Temple, and Canon of Lichfield. He had also held the livings of Piddleton and Shrivenham, and at the time of his appointment to the Principality he was Rector of St. Bartholomew's in the City of London, a living which he held to his death. Yet, in spite of the distinguished position he held, he appears to have excited little except contempt and ridicule at Oxford. Perhaps no better phrase can be found to describe his mental defects than that of Dr. Prideaux, to whom he was " a man of a magotty brain, and a singular method of conduct from all mankind beside." In all the copious Oxford papers of the seventeenth century, it is difficult to find a single good word that was said of him outside the realm of obituary notices. Dr. Prideaux in especial, who was Canon with him at Christchurch, delighted to keep a diary of his numerous follies, which he used to describe in letters to John Ellis—how he " raged most furiously " because the servants of Christchurch had taken away the joint from the table before he appeared; how he "could scarcely be dissuaded from beating a servant" who served Dr. Pocock before him. He recommends John Ellis to go and hear him preach at the Temple "if he had a mind to hear some of his nonsense." These sermons of his were an especial annoyance to Dr. Prideaux.

He maliciously relates how Dr. Woodroffe used a

sermon which he had preached on the death of the Duke of York's coachman for a deceased alderman of Oxford. In this same sermon he is credited with having recommended "godfathers to present their godsons with winding-sheets at birth in order to put them in mind of their mortality." Another of his sermons was "the most scandalous duncecall sermon that hath been preached before the University ever since the King's return, as it is agreed on by all that heard it." His relations with women exposed him to equal ridicule.

"Last night" (we are told) "he had Madam Walcup at his lodgings, and stood with her in the great window next the quadrangle, where he was seen by Mr. Dean himself, and almost all the house, toyeing with her most ridiculously, and fanning himself with her fan for almost all the afternoon."

He was shrewdly suspected of fortune-hunting. He married the sister of Sir Blewet Stonehouse, who was reputed to be worth £3,000; but Dr. Prideaux thought the family were "too cunning to be cheated by Woodruffe," and as for the money promised, "he must get it where he can." Whether he got it or not is not recorded; but the marriage took place, and Dr. Woodroffe became a wealthy man. The £3,000 caused no rupture in the family, as is shown by the fact that George Stonehouse, the heir to the baronetcy, was one of the earliest pupils of the Doctor at Gloucester Hall. It is not quite easy at this date to account for these tokens of animosity. The accounts that have been preserved of him are mostly from the pens of his political opponents, and written in days when political animosity was most violent. Even his worst enemies were compelled to acknowledge the vigour and scholarship of Dr. Woodroffe, and it was held that he was "not soe unfit a man for the Bishoprick of Oxford as some apprehend." But the truth probably is that he had a passion for self-advertisement at a time when self-advertisement was still unpopular. It was felt that his success in life was due rather to his scheming than to merit, and in the staid and oligarchic life of Oxford of that day he appeared little better than an adventurer. It is a significant fact, pointing to jealousy as the chief cause for the general dislike felt for him, that in the last years of his life, when his canonry was sequestrated, when his Hall was empty and his Greek College had proved a hopeless failure, when he himself had suffered imprisonment in the Fleet, the storm of obloquy almost entirely ceases.

But whatever he may have been as a man, there is no doubt that Worcester men owe him a deep debt of gratitude. He restored the Hall when it was practically a desert, and the very existence of the College must be attributed in no small measure to his pertinacity and courage. Nothing could well have been more dismal than the aspect of Gloucester Hall on his assuming office. During the past eleven years there had been only three matriculations at the Hall, and none at all in the last four. Dr. Byrom Eaton, at the time of his resignation, had long been non-resident, and the great storm of January 12, 1690, had added to the desolation which Loggan's sketch of 1675 so forcibly depicts. Within a week of his entry the workmen were put in to repair the Hall, and the magnitude of the repairs that were necessary is shown by the fact that one writer describes it as a "rebuilding" of Gloucester Hall. The cost of the repairs was, according to one account, £40, and to another £20, a week. Unfortunately, there are no means of knowing their precise nature, and all traces of them were doubtless obliterated during the extensive building operations of the eighteenth century. Wood tells us that,

"being a man of generous and public spirit, he bestowed several hundred pounds in repairing the place, and making it a fit habitation for the Muses, which being done he, by his great interest among the gentry, made it flourish with hopeful sprouts."

Unfortunately, the "hopeful sprouts" came up very slowly. The first was a Frenchman; the next two were respectively a son, aged ten, and a nephew, aged fifteen, of the Principal. 1694 saw four matriculations, and 1695 nine. The Hall reached its zenith in 1697 with eleven matriculations and one migration, and this state of affairs was fairly well maintained till the end of the century; but in 1701 there were no matriculations, and seldom more than two or three till the end of his Principality, and at the date of his death there was hardly one scholar inside the Hall. But from the moment of his assumption of office in 1692, he was keenly interested in another scheme, which is one of the most interesting experiments in the history of the University and of the English Church. This was the establishment of a College at Oxford of boys belonging to the Greek Church, with the object of promoting the union of Christendom.

There have been two or three great movements in this direction in the history of the English Church. The first began in 1616, and persisted for nearly a century; the second began in the first half of the present century. The increase in the trade between England and the Levant under Queen Elizabeth was doubtless the cause of the desire for a closer connection between the English and Greek Churches. With this end in view, Cyril Lucar, Patriarch of Alexandria, sent Metrophanes Critopoulos, a child of noble birth and talents, to Archbishop Abbot to be educated in 1616. Archbishop Abbot forthwith "planted this generous young shoot of a Grecian school in a pleasant garden, where he may flourish amongst us, and in good time bring forth good fruit." In Oxford he "bred him full five years, with good allowance for diet, clothes, books, chamber, and other necessaries, so that his expense since his coming into England doth amount almost to £300."

"At Michaelmas last I sent for him" (he says) "to Lambeth; but by the ill counsel of somebody, he desired to go to the Court at Newmarket that he might see the King. But then he was put into a conceit that he might get something to buy him books to carry home to the Patriarch. The means that he gaped after were such as you can hardly believe, as first that he should have a knight to be made for his sake, and then a baronet."

He was quite willing to share the baronet with someone else. At length, to satisfy his desire, he bought him new out of the shops many of the Greek authors, and Chrysostom's eight tomes, and so he was to be shipped by sea with the tomes to Constantinople. But unfortunately the "generous shoot," who by this time had been converted into a "stray sheep," took up with some other Greeks, and "in a brief writing and kind of epistle," he told the Archbishop that he would rather lose his books, suffer imprisonment, and loss of life than go home in any ship. Fortunately, he was not required to do anything of the kind. The Archbishop turned him out of doors, and then in the kindness of his heart paid his passage to Constantinople. The "generous shoot" apparently spent the viaticum in London. At last he found his way to Nuremberg, with eight volumes of Chrysostom for his only luggage, and from there he wrote a splendidly imaginative letter to his Patriarch. "Gondomar had sought to debauch him, and send him to Rome; failing in this attempt, he had sought to take his life." The Patriarch was scarcely deceived; but perhaps for the credit of the scheme, Metrophanes Critopoulos was well received on his return to the East, and he subsequently became Patriarch of Alexandria. Archbishop Abbot never ceased to lament the Chrysostom, and he did not care to repeat the experiment. But, in spite of the partial failure of this first attempt, there is ample evidence that the scheme of a Greek College at Oxford was often discussed. Distinguished prelates of the Greek Church paid visits to the University, and on our side the project of reunion was warmly supported by men like Thomas Smith, of Magdalen College, and the Rev. Edward Stephens.

It is difficult to fix the date of the first definite scheme for the establishment of a College at Oxford; but there is reason to suppose that the first proposals came from the Greek Church itself. Under date July, 1677, Wood says that there was "a great talk of converting Gloucester Hall into a College for the education of 20 or 30 Greeks in Academical learning, and to send them home, but these only wanted pelf." He connects the scheme with the name of Joseph Georgirenes, Archbishop of Samos, and subsequently minister of the Greek Church in Soho, who was then on a visit to Oxford. Georgirenes followed up his visit with a petition to the Archbishop of Canterbury, in which he makes a definite suggestion that

"about twelve scholars out of Greece be constantly here, to be instructed and grounded in the true doctrine of the Church of England, whereby, with the blessing of God, they may be able dispensers thereof, and so returne into Greece aforesaid to preache the same, by whiche means your petitioner conceives the said people may be edified."

He complains that the Greeks are being prohibited

"the use of public schooles, and reduced to poverty by the tyranny of the Turks, and also grown into so great ignorance by the corruption of their Church, which daily groweth more and more corrupted, that that famous nation is in great danger of being utterly lost."

He ends the letter with a plea that some yearly revenue be appropriated to the purpose. We know nothing as to the fate of this appeal, but it was fifteen years from the time the scheme of turning Gloucester Hall into a Greek College was first mooted, before any attempt was made to carry the plan into execution. It appears that Benjamin Woodroffe had from the first formed the design of using Gloucester Hall for this purpose, and it is quite possible that he was appointed with this end in view. In October, 1692, only six weeks after he was admitted Principal, we read that "Dr. Woodroffe is erecting a new College at Oxford to be called the Greek College, and that 20 famous Grecians are sent from Antioch and Constantinople to reside there." He had already, on August 30 of that year, appeared in person before the Board of the Levant Company, and requested them to provide a free passage for any youths who might come over. To this date probably belongs a paper entitled "A Model of a College to be Settled in the University for the Education of some Youths of the Greek Church." The paper may have been written by Dr. Woodroffe himself. A similar paper, presented to Sir Thomas Cookes, entitled "A Model of a College" (the College being in this case Worcester College), reveals a similarity of authorship. Here the Greek scheme is for the first time elaborated in full. The College is to consist of twenty youths, who are to remain five years or less in Oxford, and four are to return to Greece every year, and be replaced by four others. The youths are to be from fourteen to twenty years of age, and it was desired that as many as possible should be acquainted with Turkish, Arabic, Persian, Armenian, or Russian. This may possibly point to some scheme for paying the expenses of their board by giving lessons in the Oriental languages. On their arrival they are to be delivered, either by the Governor or the Deputy-Governor of the Turkey Company, into the hands of their Governor, who having received them, shall forthwith present them to the Bishop of London, and in a day or two after conduct them to the University. They are to be divided into two classes, and their chambers shall be so arranged that they are within call of their tutor, who shall keep them to the language they are to converse in; this language for the first two years shall be Ancient Greek, and the next two Latin, and then they shall proceed to Hebrew. They must all alike be habited in the gravest sort of habit worn in their own country, and must not go out without leave of the Governor, nor without a companion, to compensate for which restraint places for innocent exercises and recreations may be allotted " within themselves." There shall be no vacation, but relaxations shall be left to the discretion of the Governor. They are to study Aristotle and the Greek scholiasts, and the controversial theology between Greece and Rome. There are to be two tutors in addition to the Governor. Their solemn devotions are to be at half-past five in the morning, half an hour before supper, and at nine at night. They are to dispute twice a term in Greek in the schools, and are to learn an orthodox catechism which is to be compiled for their especial benefit. A report of their progress is to be written yearly, and presented to the Bishop of London and the Turkey Company. The College is to be carried on by voluntary subscriptions, and trustees and auditors are to be appointed.

In spite of these preparations, the scheme seems to have hung fire at first. Either no scholars, or very few scholars, came over. The Oxford wits derided the scheme, and in June, 1693, some Latin verses were written in which Gloucester Hall was compared, very much to its disadvantage, with Rump Hall, an alehouse half a mile north of St. Giles. The first four lines, which are here given, are the best, and are sufficiently descriptive of the character of the verses, which extend to sixteen lines. They are as follows:

"Dum pergræcatur parvæ chorus ebrius aulæ,
  Ah! major Græcis indiget aula suis;
  Hinc ait insultans vulgus Rumpense 'Calendas
  Induct ad Græcas Græca juventa togam.'"

The ill-success of the scheme doubtless induced Dr. Woodroffe to write a letter to Callinicus, the Patriarch of Constantinople, asking for pupils. It has been often thought that this letter represents the commencement of the Greek College, and we certainly have no definite information as to Greek scholars previous to its composition in 1694. But it is not likely that Dr. Woodroffe would have signed himself, as he does in that letter, "President and head of the Greek College," unless there had been some pupils actually *in esse*. The letter practically is a repetition, with many of the details omitted, of the "Model of a College," to which we have already referred. The following points of difference may, however, be noted. Medicine and mathematics are added to the scheme of studies. The places from which the youths are to come are definitely specified; there are to be about five from each patriarchate—that is to say, from Constantinople, Alexandria, Antioch, and Jerusalem. It is suggested that Englishmen in the East should pay the expenses of their passage to England, and it is provided that their actual equipment should be placed in the hands of the three British priests who respectively resided at Constantinople, Aleppo, and Hierapolis.

In spite of this letter, one still fails to get any information as to the actual presence of Greek youths in Oxford, and there is no certain trace of their arrival till about 1698. On March 1 in that year

Dr. Woodroffe advised the Levant Company that some youths had actually arrived, and requested the Company to look after them until he had made arrangements for their reception. A fortnight later the Company voted £40 to defray the travelling expenses of five youths who had arrived from Smyrna.

The full scheme was in all probability never carried out. The number of youths in the College probably never exceeded ten, and from various sources we have only been able to recover the names of ten as present in Oxford during the whole of the thirteen years that the College nominally existed. In all such schemes the financial work generally presents the greatest difficulty; the enthusiasm of the earlier supporters is apt to cool very rapidly, especially when, as happened in this case, the scheme is not an unqualified success. The first idea was to support the College by voluntary subscriptions from the English in Turkey, and those who were interested in the College in England; but there is no evidence that any considerable sum of money was received in this way. It is difficult to understand why the Greeks were not asked to contribute to their own support. The only Greek scholar about whom we have any definite information was a son of one of the noblest families in Corcyra, and he certainly had plenty of money. But from the first it was taken for granted that the Greeks would be supported at the public expense. Under these circumstances Dr. Woodroffe appealed to the Treasury for support in May, 1700, and his appeal was backed by the Bishop of London. On May 28 the appeal was considered, and the petitioners were ordered to inquire whether any lands had been left for superstitious uses, and if there were any such, " his Majesty would consider of it." In the following month the Bishop of London writes to Mr. Lowndes, the Secretary of the Treasury, and informs him that an estate called Ecclesdale, in Lancashire, had been given to superstitious uses. He entreated the Secretary to lay the matter before the Board in the interests of the Greek youths at Oxford. The matter came before the Board, and was referred to the Attorney and Surveyor to advise on title. Meanwhile, on June 25, the King gave the College £100, " but no more afterwards," and the donation was acknowledged in a fulsome preface to a volume which Dr. Woodroffe published at this date. No more was done in the reign of William III., but on July 8, 1702, Dr. Woodroffe sent to the Treasury an account of the charges he had been at for the Greek youths at Gloucester Hall. These amounted to £1,105, which he sought might be reimbursed to him, or, in the alternative, that a prosecution which the Government had instituted against him in reference to some duties on some salt mines in Cheshire, of which he was proprietor, might be stayed. This account bears the endorsement, " My Lord will speak with ye Bishop of London." In November of the following year he sent in another petition—first, for an establishment for the Greek youths, to the number of ten, to receive their education according to the Church of England; secondly, that several of them having been above three years under the care and at the sole charge of Dr. Woodroffe, excepting £200 received of the Royal Bounty, there might be a supply for the same amounting to about £1,100; thirdly, that prosecution might be stayed for

£1,100 for the duty on rock-salt in Cheshire, which amounted to many thousands a year. The cost of the youths could not be less than £300 or £400 a year. Dr. Woodroffe artfully supported this appeal by a description of the arts which the Roman Catholic agents had employed in order to decoy the youths away from the College. This appeal to the Protestant feelings of the Queen was doubtless the cause of the success of the petition, for she granted all his prayers. The forfeited estate of Ecclesdale in Lancashire, which had belonged to one Dickenson, was appropriated for the purposes of the College. It was estimated that it would give each of the ten scholars between £30 and £40 a year. In spite of his apparent success, Dr. Woodroffe does not seem to have been much better off, for two years later, in July, 1705, he writes again. The arrears of payment have by this time risen from £1,100 to £2,000, in spite of payments out of the Royal Bounty; and he still owed £600 for duty on rock-salt, a debt which he requested might be taken out of the arrears.

Some papers of about this date in the Treasury referring to a forfeited Dickenson estate may perhaps serve to explain why it was that Dr. Woodroffe reaped no benefit from the apparent munificence of Queen Anne. It appears that "William Diccenson," at the time of the forfeiture, had assigned his lands to his creditors for the payment of his debts, and this would effectually bar any proceedings by the Treasury. We get another reference to the Dickenson estate in 1706 after the Greek College had failed, and this shows that another grantee of the estate, Mr. William Palmes, one of the most importunate beggars who ever plagued a Treasury for help which he did not deserve, had looked into the estate, and could make nothing out of it. The only connection between the Dickenson estate assigned to the Greek College, and the Dickenson estate that was assigned to creditors, is that of name and time, but there is no reason why the estates should not be the same.

If so, the whole affair affords a good illustration of the method in which finance was conducted in the reign of Queen Anne. To satisfy an importunate suitor, to get rid of a profitless estate, and to avoid a troublesome litigation by one and the same stroke of business, is a fine example of the niggardliness of the Treasury of the day. The reply to this last petition was not so favourable as was that to its predecessor, in spite of the fact that Dr. Woodroffe had been employing the interval in fulsome comparisons between Queen Anne and the Queen of Sheba.

> " Comes Sheba's wealthy Queen, but what can we
> Poor Grecian youths bring as our gifts to thee?
> Our poverty, great Queen, is all's our own,
> And this the greatest present to the throne."

"The Queen would do what she had promised, but there must be no deductions out of the salt duty."

A little later in the year there was another urgent appeal. By this time £400 in all had been received out of the Royal Bounty. But the Doctor was still £1,400 to the bad in respect of the College, and £600 in debt for the duty on rock-salt. More Greek youths were coming in, and if process were now to go against him, "he and the good work would be utterly ruined, the honour of the nation and religion must suffer, and occasion be thereby given to the scornings and insultings of the enemies of our faith, who are so ready to snatch away the honour of so good a work from us."

It appears that nothing had come in from the forfeited estates, and in January of the following year the arrears had amounted to between two and three thousand pounds. The Treasury replied by directing a stay of process in respect to the rock-salt till the following Michaelmas, 1706, and this is the last we hear of the relations of Dr. Woodroffe with the Treasury. Whether in the end he was compelled to pay the £600 for rock-salt, and whether he received his arrears, is left in doubt; but we do know that shortly afterwards, from a variety of causes, he was involved in such a complication of financial troubles that he became a prisoner in the Fleet.

We must now go back a few years to consider the internal condition of the College, which was almost as unfortunate as its financial history. At first all went very well. "Those who came first were well enough ordered for some time," and Dr. Woodroffe formed the most extravagant expectations as to the future success of his pupils, and the wide-reaching influence that was to be exercised by the Greek College. An address of Dr. Woodroffe to the Greek students about this time is recorded by Francis Prossalentes, one of the pupils of the Hall:

"Calling us together, he began to speak in this way: 'I fear, my dear children, when I hear you wish to go back into your own country. Be strong then in the faith you have learnt; do not cast away the truth which you have found. For God lives and our Queen through whom you will have the greater honour in the Eastern Church. You, sir (addressing me), will occupy the seat of Constantine ("Heaven forefend!" interpolates Prossalentes), and you the Patriarchate of Alexandria, and another that of Jerusalem, and another that of Antioch, and the rest of you the most reputable places in your chief cities.'"

But the Greeks complained at an early date that the teaching given them was altogether disorderly and unmethodical.

"First they would learn grammar for a few days, then physics for five or six, then logic, then grammar again, then mathematics—in short, in the space of five or six months they read all branches of knowledge and exhausted none of them.'

But the gravest accusation of all was that Dr. Woodroffe deliberately tried to subvert their faith, and to wean them from the doctrines of the Greek Church. It is impossible to regard this as anything else than a breach of faith. The Eastern Church would never have allowed them to come to England if this had been the object in view.

Matters reached a climax in 1704. Dr. Woodroffe no doubt thought that it was time to give some example of the proficiency which the Greeks had attained in their studies. So he published a controversial tract on the sufficiency of the sacred writings. The tract took the form of a dialogue, in which he conversed with two of his scholars, George Aptal and George Maroules, and convinced them of the uselessness of the faith in tradition which forms an integral part of the Greek creed.

He wound up the tract with a poem in honour of Queen Anne, in which the Greek scholars are made to dilate upon the wonderful resemblance between Queen Anne and the Queen of Sheba; and lest perchance she should not understand Greek, an English translation is added. He then called upon the Greek scholars as a body to sign the paper in token of their agreement with its views. Seven of them did this, namely, Simon Homer, George Aptal, George Maroules, Stephen Constantine, George Homer, Michael Damiral, and John Aptal. But one of them, Francis Prossalentes, to whom we have already referred, flatly refused to do so. As an immediate consequence, very likely of this refusal, he fled to Amsterdam, and from the safe retreat afforded by that city he composed a tract attacking Dr. Woodroffe, and refuting his arguments against traditions. The title of the work is, "The Heretic Teacher confuted by his Orthodox Disciple: a Book very useful to the Orthodox confirming Traditions, and exposing the Sophistries of Benjamin Woodroff, the Teacher of the Greek College in Britain." Each of these works is excessively rare. The British Museum does not possess a copy of Woodroffe's work, and the Bodleian does not possess a copy of the work of Prossalentes. Both of them are in the same dialectical form. In the former all the arguments in favour, and in the latter all the arguments against, traditions are completely overthrown. They can hardly be recommended for modern perusal. But the tract of Prossalentes was thought to be of sufficient interest in Greece to deserve a reprint, and a second edition was published in Athens in 1862, edited by Paul Dameros, with a biographical introduction (to which we are indebted) by A. Moustoxudos.

Having forged his thunderbolt, Prossalentes proceeded to launch it at the head of Dr. Woodroffe. He apparently presented every member of the Greek College with the book, and Hearne saw a copy in the possession of one of them. He relates with some gusto that "he falls upon Dr. Woodroffe very smartly." It must have been a poor return to poor Dr. Woodroffe for all his labour, anxiety and hospitality to be held up to contumely throughout the Churches of the East as a heretic, and to have his own pupils turned against him by this polemic of a former pupil. We can scarcely acquit Prossalentes of a charge of the basest ingratitude. His subsequent career may be briefly told, because in all probability it is representative of the fate of most of the members of the Greek College. He was twenty-seven at the time when he wrote the pamphlet against Dr. Woodroffe. He soon afterwards returned to his native country, and was ordained a priest in the Greek Church. He ministered for the greater part of his life in Corcyra, but latterly he retired to Zacynthos. He appears to have been a man of some eloquence, and his Lenten sermons in particular attracted considerable attention. His father, a doctor, Hippolytus, and his mother, Sapphira, occupied a prominent position on the island, and his attachment to the ministry was regarded as no small sacrifice of temporal prospects. He died on September 5, 1725.

But this was the least of the internal difficulties of the College. The Greek youths appeared to wander almost as soon as they arrived. We find the Levant

Company allowing twenty-five dollars passage-money to each of two Greek youths who wished to return home as early as 1702, and they were allowed to take their books with them. In the same year two of the Greek youths were persuaded by a third, named Stephen Constantine, at the instigation, it was said, of a person belonging to the Portugal Ambassador's Chapel, to leave the College, where, if the truth must be told, they probably suffered considerable hardship and privation; and with that propensity for wandering about the Continent of Europe which seems to have been ingrained in the Greek youths who were sent to study in Oxford, took ship to Holland. Here they were provided with money, and kindly received by the people of the place. These same persons took them to the Hague, and from that point it was proposed that they should go by boat to Middelburg.* When they were out at sea they found they were steering quite an opposite course. To their remonstrances the master of the vessel replied that he was taking them whither he had orders to take them, and eventually brought them to Antwerp, and here the whole horrible plot was revealed. Stephen Constantine appears as an emissary of the Pope, who had for three years sold himself and his brethren to the Papal agents. He now assumed command of the expedition, and pulled out of his pocket a purse from the Governor of Flanders. On landing they were met by three priests, who were to take care of them, and who attended them to Mechlin, and thence to Louvain,

* A difficulty in the narrative is that Middelburg is an inland town close to Flushing, and so far as it could be was on the way to Antwerp.

where they were presented to the Internuncio of the Pope. The Internuncio was disappointed, and expected to find Homer, the eldest of the Greek scholars at the Hall, among the number; but he told them that a great sum of money was ready for their use, and the Pope had provided for their coming for the last three years. And now

"they began to deal plainly with them, greately exclaiming against the English as the worst of heretics, and telling them that they were to renounce all their errors, and to be instructed that they might be received into the true Catholic Church. In order whereunto they were put into the Irish College, and often disputed with to be convinced of their errors, but that not prevailing, they were told that his Holiness had a desire to see them, and to Rome they must goe, where they should find what it was to offend an Apostolic minister. And so they were sent to Paris, where the Pope's Nuncio entertained them beyond what they had ever seen, and a letter of grace came to them from his Holiness written in Greek. They had desired to have had some new cloths, but twas denyed, they being told that his Holiness had a great desire to see them in their own countrey habit, meaning the habit they wore here in England, and had travelled in, and are now returned in the same to London."

From Paris they were sent to Avignon, and from thence to Marseilles, whence they were shipped for Civita Vecchia; but the master on touching at Genoa, gave them leave to walk about the streets, and so they found out the English Consul, and told him that they were under Her Majesty's protection, and that they were now being sent to Rome to be put in the Inquisition, and they therefore begged his protection. The Consul, having withstood all the endeavours of the Romanists to recover them, shipped them for Leghorn, from whence, by the favour of the Consul there, they were put on board an English ship, in which they eventually arrived at the port of London.

Such is the story as recorded by an anonymous hand in the State Papers. But there are two other accounts of a similar transaction written by the Rev. Edward Stephens. The first is practically identical with that given above, and would almost lead one to suppose that the two accounts were by the same hand. The second apparently relates to the same transaction, but it contains some remarkable points of difference.

"About the same time" (says Stephens) "happened another occasion to manifest the indefensibleness of their cause by a letter sent from Rome to a young Grecian scholar then with me. It was delivered by an English or Irish gentleman belonging to the Envoy of Florence, and probably a priest, who would have persuaded him to have gone to Rome. But he sent him such a letter of objections, that this gentleman would never after discourse with him. Meanwhile that young Grecian and his brother were trapped into the hands of the Internuncio at Brussels by the means of one belonging to the Envoy of Portugal."

In this account the two students were represented as stopping with the Rev. Edward Stephens, and no mention at all is made of the nefarious designs of Stephen Constantine. It is extremely difficult to know what to think of the whole story. The name of the Rev. Edward Stephens throws suspicion on any relation of Papal designs. The doubts that contemporaries felt as to his sanity are strengthened, if not confirmed, by a perusal of his numerous controversial writings. The Roman Catholic Church and its schemes were to him almost a monomania. It is difficult to understand what advantage the Roman Church could expect to have reaped from the forcible conversion of a couple of Greek youngsters. On the other hand may be set the well-known imaginative powers of the Greek youth, their notorious ill-treatment at the Greek College, their knowledge that any story of Papal designs would win a ready acceptance from Woodroffe and Stephens, and we arrive at what to some at any rate appears a more likely version. The ill-usage, neglect, and confinement at the Oxford College induced two or three of them to run away. That they were not absolutely without means is shown by the case of Francis Prossalentes. They wandered about Europe till their means were exhausted, and then appealed to the compassion and the credulity of the English Consul, who sent them back to College. Here they found Woodroffe not at all anxious to scrutinize too closely a story which was in all probability the immediate means of obtaining for him substantial advances from the Treasury. When they professed that "their faith was still unscathed," thy probably won applause for their sufferings in the cause. Another difficulty in the story is the part of Stephen Constantine the apostate. It is hardly likely that he would have been received again into the College, if the story told of him is true, yet we find him a signatory of the pamphlet of 1704.

On their arrival in England the three were arrested for a debt of £27 in respect of their passage from Leghorn, and they were only released on payment of the debt by the Levant Company. Two of them were then sent back to Greece in November, 1709, and the Company advanced twenty-five dollars to each of them for their passage. Of course, it is possible to accept the story of Papal machinations, but we for our part prefer the contemporary version, that he "used the poor Greek boys in such a manner that they all, or most of them, ran away from him"; or the account given in another contemporary pamphlet, that

"they were so ill-accommodated, both for their studies and other necessaries, that some of them stayed not many months, and others would have gone if they had known how, and there are now but two left here, one being come lately thence to London."

From this point the record of the College is one of disaster. A rival institution was started at Halle, in Saxony, "where very good provision was made for the Greeks, so that they lived very comfortably." The French King started a similar College on Papal lines in Paris. Even in England there were some thoughts of starting a rival house. Three more pupils were shipped back to Greece by the Levant Company free of charge in 1704, and one more in 1705. The anonymous author of "A Good and Necessary Proposal for the Restitution of Catholic Communion between the Greek Churches and the Churches of England" suggested that there was no need of a College, but "of a good house, well situated, and with convenient lodging for some Greek clergymen and young scholars, and a decent oratory here in London." A subscription was started to effect this end, and there are some slight indications that such a house was actually started. Moreover, the escapades of the Greek scholars in England had attracted the attention of the authorities at Constantinople. The result was a letter written by the registrar of the Greek Church, Jeremiah Xantheus, to the Rev. Edward Stephens, in which he says that

"the irregular life of certain priests and laymen of the Eastern Church living in London is a matter of great concern to the Church; wherefore the Church forbids any to go and study at Oxford, be they ever so willing."

This was in 1705. But Grecians still lingered on at Gloucester Hall, at any rate till 1707, and there are no means of saying when the last departed. An extract from a manuscript in the library of the University of Zittau may form a fitting conclusion to a somewhat fantastic story. One day in 1725 there came into the library at Zittau a Greek traveller, who had resided in Italy, Paris, London, Oxford, St. Petersburg, Lubeck, Hamburg, Halle, Leipsic, Dresden, and Zittau. He pronounced an opinion on the manuscript he was shown, which was considered learned "for a traveller." He spoke, and then, as the writer tells the story, "he disappeared." Was this mysterious student one of Dr. Woodroffe's pupils still wandering among the Universities of Europe?

There is one other matter in connection with the scheme which may be mentioned. All this time Dr. Woodroffe had been negotiating with Sir Thomas Cookes and his trustees in reference to the foundation of Worcester College. No doubt one very considerable objection to the plan was that Gloucester Hall was already appropriated to the Greeks, and it was probably to meet this difficulty that Dr. Woodroffe began building a separate habitation for them on a plot of ground on a site which is at present represented by the bottom of Beaumont Street, and immediately opposite the gates of the College. The site is marked on old maps of Oxford as an irregular quadrangular piece of land, with a building at two of the corners. Here he erected a large building, incorporating into it the last remains of Beaumont Palace. But it was built of such slight materials, that it was thought it could not stand very long; and for that reason, at first at any rate, nobody ever presumed to lodge in it. It lasted, however, till 1806, and was then pulled down, a valuation of £401 16s. being paid to St. John's College, the freeholders of the site. And thus for nearly a century the only memorial that Oxford had before its eyes of the Greek scheme was a building that went by the name of " Woodroffe's Folly."

CHAPTER VIII
1696—1714

THE FOUNDATION OF WORCESTER COLLEGE

But while all hopes as to the success of the Greek College were rapidly disappearing, Dr. Woodroffe was busying himself with another scheme, which was ultimately to convert Gloucester Hall into Worcester College. About the year 1696 Sir Thomas Cookes, a baronet of Bentley Pauncefote in the county of Worcester, first conceived the idea of devoting £10,000 towards the foundation of a College at Oxford. A few months later he was rash enough to confide his project to a relative, one Willmot, all unconscious that in so doing he was condemning himself for the rest of his life to the incessant teasings of fortune-hunting dons. From Willmot Dr. Woodroffe got wind of the scheme. He at once came to the conclusion that Gloucester Hall was the right place for the endowment, and on June 25 he wrote to convince Sir Thomas Cookes of the fact. His first hope was to gain possession of the money by a bold assault. He took it for granted that Sir Thomas was going to endow the Hall, though he had expressed no intention of the kind, and sought to place him in such a position that he could not well retire from the plan. By the end of July he had prepared a "Model of a College," for which he had no doubt found the "Model of the Greek College" useful. By August 5 he extracted a reply, somewhat ambiguous in its terms, from Sir Thomas, who professed "to have a passion for Gloucester Hall, and that it stood rather above than level with any other College in his thoughts." This half-hearted welcome only spurred Dr. Woodroffe on to keener exertions. In four days more the "Model of the College" was in the hands of Sir Thomas. Then Sir Thomas replied with a request for information as to the probable cost of the scheme drawn up by Dr. Woodroffe, and he is said to have added that, "living or dying," he intended to endow Gloucester Hall.

Having obtained this very satisfactory avowal, Dr. Woodroffe should have given Sir Thomas a little breathing-space. But he was unable to see that the very weakness of will which had led Sir Thomas to surrender to Dr. Woodroffe's first assault might at any time lead him to revoke his surrender, and to break his word. Dr. Woodroffe's subsequent proceedings were of a character to alarm a benefactor who required the very gentlest treatment. There were several pieces of land in the immediate vicinity of Gloucester Hall in the market, with a total rental of £50 a year. Dr. Woodroffe felt so sure of his benefactor that he actually purchased them for £1,300 before he had gone through the formality of obtaining Sir Thomas's consent. The result was an immediate coolness on the part of Sir Thomas. He gave the Doctor to understand that he had not got the £10,000 to bestow at that date, and that the money would have to be recovered from certain creditors. Meanwhile Dr. Woodroffe airily avowed that as Sir Thomas would not take the land, he would buy it himself.

The rest of 1697 and the early part of 1698 were spent by the Doctor in the composition of statutes and charters. The history is somewhat mysterious. Apparently there were five drafts, all differing from each other in the most important particulars, and the one that finally passed the Privy Seal was one that had been approved by no one except Dr. Woodroffe. Two copies of these charters are in the Bodleian, one exists in the library of Lambeth Palace, and one in the Record Office. They were all equally valueless, and a comparison of their various demerits is scarcely important. It may be to this period that the story of an abortive charter belongs which records that Dr. Woodroffe inserted a clause empowering the Sovereign to put in and turn out Fellows at his will. With the recent precedent of Magdalen College in their minds, men were not likely to accede to such a proposal. But it is more likely that this clause, if it ever existed, was drafted at a period subsequent to the death of Sir Thomas, as otherwise it would almost certainly have been mentioned by Dr. Baron.

At length, on October 22, 1698, a charter for the foundation of Worcester College passed the Privy Seal. It began with a recital of the picturesque but erroneous legends which were then so much in vogue as to the origin of the University. It tells of the various changes and losses which the Hall had suffered in process of

FOUNDATION OF WORCESTER COLLEGE 157

time, without, however, losing the name of a College "in which for many centuries it delighted." It refers to that noble *generale studium* which flourished at Cricklade ere ever the Saxons came to these isles, while still the Britons bore sway. It speaks of the chapel and the library which had excited the envy of all beholders. Then came the lamentable period when the College was changed *in gladiorum bombardarumque fabricas,* as though it was henceforth to be consecrated rather to Vulcan than to Pallas.

"And now" (it continues) "our faithful and well-beloved subject, Benjamin Woodroffe, has informed us what great services that Hall has done to Church and State, and how, even in recent times, it has nourished men who were remarkable for their humanity and liberality, and so it pleases us to lend assent to so pious and laudable a design. Know, then, all men, now and to come, that we give and concede to the aforesaid Benjamin Woodroffe every liberty and power to do all things necessary for promoting so good a work. In the first place, it is our will that the aforesaid College shall be, and become henceforth, a free College, by the name of Worcester College, and that the said Benjamin Woodroffe shall be the first and only Governor thereof, under the title of Provost; further, that there be twelve Fellows thereof, of whom six shall be senior and six junior, and also eight scholars."

The most remarkable point about the charter is that it makes absolutely no reference to Sir Thomas Cookes, and that to all appearance Dr. Woodroffe is not only perpetual Provost and Corporation in one, but also Founder. To this charter was added a body of statutes, which bears all the characteristics of Dr. Woodroffe's unpractical genius. They were passed on November 18, 1698. The preamble states that they were drawn up by Sir Thomas Cookes, with the advice and help of the Archbishop of Canterbury and the Bishop of Worcester, together with that of Dr. Woodroffe. This is obviously untrue. The only thing the Archbishop and Bishop had done was to sign an earlier and different draft of the statutes, while Sir Thomas had not only refused to sign the statutes at all, but had shown himself unwilling to part with his money, without which the statutes were entirely nugatory.

The statutes themselves are remarkable not only for their extraordinarily monastic spirit, but also for the magnitude and breadth of the scheme of education which the slender sum of £500 a year was to set on foot. The Provost and Fellows were to have control of the endowments. Two of the senior Fellows were to be nominated in the case of a vacancy in the Provostship, and of these two one was to be appointed to that office by the Chancellor of the University. Preference to the schools of Bromsgrove and Feckenham was to be given in the election of scholars; and in default of scholars from these schools, Worcester and Hartlebury were to have the preference. Founder's kin were to be entitled to election, and after Founder's kin the charity boys of the various schools who were clothed *cœrulea veste*. Founder's kin could be elected to Fellowships after two, and other scholars after four, years' residence in the College.

Marriage was forbidden, and the Fellows were to take Holy Orders, though two might be laymen, of whom one might be a student of medicine, and one of

Civil Law, or, if necessary, both might study Civil Law. No one was to retain his Fellowship for more than twenty years without the leave of the Founder, if alive, or of the visitor, at the request of the Provost and the majority of the Fellows, after the Founder was dead. The Provost and one or two of the Fellows were to elect to scholarships and hold an examination, at which the Dean of Worcester, and the incumbents of the parishes in which the schools were situated, were to preside. Five lectures were to be established—two *solemnes* in theology and history, which were to be held in the chapel; and three ordinary in mathematics, philosophy, and philology.

The theological lecture was not to be on the Cookes Foundation; it was to be purely catechetical, and similar in all respects to that founded by Richard Busby at Balliol. Though it is not expressly stated, it is clear that certain funds bequeathed by Richard Busby, the headmaster of Westminster, were expected to meet this charge. Dr. Woodroffe, as an Old Westminster, would doubtless be well known to Richard Busby, and during the last years of his life Busby had apparently supported both a catechetical and a mathematical lecturer at Gloucester Hall, and he expressed a wish to endow a catechetical lecture if Dr. Woodroffe would accept the same. An attempt was made to carry this scheme into effect in the administration suit that followed on Busby's death.

On February 20, 1698, a decree was made to the effect that "his trustees, if they should think fit, might allow to a catechetical lecturer at Worcester College in Oxford, formerly Gloucester Hall, such annual sum not exceeding £20 per annum, as is allowed to the lecturer at Balliol." The endowment never came to anything, probably because the scheme to convert the Hall into a College was frustrated.

The mathematical, philosophical, and philological lecturers (the latter of whom was to lecture on Hebrew), were to lecture five, or at least four, times a week. There were to be three " courses " of anatomy, chemistry, and botany respectively. The anatomist was to give ten lectures, and was to comment on the first seven verses of the twelfth chapter of Ecclesiastes in order to explain his teaching. The chemist was to give four lectures on the principles of chemistry, and twelve on experimental chemistry. The botanist in the same way was to give four general and eight practical lectures. In the latter he must exhibit the plants to his listeners, and must take his audience four times into the fields, woods, and marshes to pick, collect, and distinguish plants.

Then followed arrangements for disputations, orations, and anniversary sermons. Chapel was to be at six in summer, and seven in winter. A Latin form of prayer was to be read, according to the use of Christchurch; but the lessons, and even the prayers, if the Provost thought fit, were to be read in Greek. The Fellows and scholars were to devote a quarter of an hour nightly to the reading of the Bible. At every meal a chapter of the Bible was to be read by an undergraduate in Greek or Latin. Attendance at Holy Communion was made compulsory on all who had passed their fifteenth year. During the life of the Founder, his name was to be mentioned at grace both before and after meals.

The financial part of the scheme was regulated to

From a photograph by the [*Oxford Camera Club*

FOUNDATION OF WORCESTER COLLEGE 161

suit the endowment of the College rather than the needs of the Fellows. Twelve Fellows and eight scholars, at £14 apiece, absorbed £280. A Vice-Provost, a sacristan, a librarian, and two moderators were to be secured for a sum amounting in all to £30. Six lecturers were to receive a sum amounting in all to £61 6s. 8d. a year. The mathematical lecturer was to be best paid, as he received £13 per annum. The three "courses" were to receive £26 in all, the botanist for his arduous duties only getting £6 per annum. *Actus solemnes* swallowed up £16 per annum. Various miscellaneous items absorbed £43. Among these were to be an oration in memory of the Founder at 13s. 4d., and criticisms of various books at £2 for each subject; £5 was allotted to philosophical experiments, and £26, the largest individual item, to exercises in Holy Scripture. Lastly, there were gratuities to those taking certain degrees which would amount to £30 a year. Thus, out of a total of £500 a year, the sum of £486 6s. 8d. was already appropriated. The balance of a little more than £13 was to pay all establishment charges, and provide the salary of the Provost, who was to receive double a Fellow's allowance.

Not more than two—and if possible not more than one—persons were to occupy the same room. Pecuniary fines for breaches of discipline were to be discouraged, and in no case were they to exceed half a Fellow's emoluments—namely, £7 out of £14 a year. If the fine proved ineffectual, the offender could be "gated" for as many days or weeks as the Provost or Vice-Provost thought fit; or he might be sentenced to a "minor excommunication, as it were," and debarred from all intercourse with his Fellows either in Hall or chapel. A public reprimand might follow upon further disobedience, and after the first or second reprimand the offender might be suspended for six months. At the end of that time, if he failed to ask pardon, his name would be wiped off the books. Elaborate pecuniary penalties were enforced for failure to attend lectures. The ordinary academical statutes were to be observed as to frequenting the houses of citizens, taverns, and other places of resort, and so on. The Bishop of Worcester, and, in case of a vacancy in the see, the Bishop of Oxford, were to be visitors after the death of Sir Thomas Cookes.

It is not possible at this date to understand why Dr. Woodroffe went to the trouble and expense of obtaining these statutes. It may be that Sir Thomas expected wonders to be done with his £10,000, and that Dr. Woodroffe was compelled to accede to every suggestion that was made. At any rate, during the year 1698 it was regarded as quite settled that the charity should go to Gloucester Hall in some shape or form, though there seem to have been all sorts of ideas as to the way in which the money would be laid out. We have another form of the same rumour which must belong to about this date in one of the Ballard letters:

"'Tis said the instruments for Worcester College are sealed, and nothing remains but ye laying out of ye money on a good purchase. Sir Thomas and his heirs are to choose one of 32 Fellows elected to be Provost. The Chancellor is to be perpetual visitor."

But, unfortunately, it was exactly at this point that there was a hitch in the negotiations. The real reason for it was that Sir Thomas Cookes had either changed his mind entirely, or had grown lukewarm as to the scheme. No doubt he was annoyed by Dr. Woodroffe's importunities, and was unwilling to part with his money. In order to find a way of escape, he had resort to several elaborate artifices. He persuaded his relatives to represent to him that it was unfair that the Founder's kin should be robbed of the right to appoint a Provost in favour of the Chancellor. On the other hand, it was not in the least likely that the Chancellor of the University would surrender his patronage of the Hall on the foundation of the College. Dr. Woodroffe had memorialized the King on the subject as early as January, 1697, and the Bishop of Oxford, who heard of the petition, wrote to Dr. Charlett to say the petition had been passed on to the Duke of Ormonde, and that he was sure his Grace would suffer nothing to be done in it but as the University should approve; and as the University would certainly refuse to remove any obstacle out of Dr. Woodroffe's path, the difficulty presented might well appear insuperable.

Such as it was, it put a complete stop to the negotiations for the space of two years. In the meantime a new and formidable competitor appeared in the person of Dr. John Baron, Fellow, and subsequently Master, of Balliol. He had originally been in favour of the Gloucester Hall scheme, and, as a confidant and relative of Sir Thomas, had been able to lend Dr. Woodroffe valuable support. It is not apparent when the change in his attitude took place. The pulpit of the parish church at Feckenham was regarded as the natural spot for fighting the matter out, and giving Sir Thomas good advice for the benefit of his soul and the advantage of the University. Hither Dr. Baron resorted on June 1, 1699, in order to preach the annual sermon to the trustees of the school at Feckenham which had been endowed by Sir Thomas. His text was taken from Gal. vi. 10 : " As we have therefore opportunity, let us do good unto all men." It does not appear whether Sir Thomas was present; but in order to obviate any difficulty of this kind, Dr. Baron published the sermon, with a dedication to the baronet. He devoted his sermon to an elaborate exposition of the two doctrines —that " men of ability " should do good " while they live," and that " those charitable settlements are best which are designed to promote and encourage learning." Needless to say, the man of ability was Sir Thomas himself. Unfortunately, there is not a word to show whether Dr. Baron was advocating the claims of Balliol or of Gloucester Hall in this sermon. But if there had been two schemes afloat, Dr. Baron would have referred to their respective advantages. On the other hand, a reference to those " who may be idly and unprofitably busy, and serve no ends but those of folly and vanity," may be intended for Dr. Woodroffe. In any case, six weeks later Sir Thomas threw out a suggestion that Balliol College should receive the endowment, and, according to Dr. Baron, this proposal was made on Sir Thomas's own initiative. On July 18 Mr. Mason wrote to Dr. Baron, on behalf of Sir Thomas, that he was resolved to settle his charity somewhere, and

" he bids me tell you Balliol College will stand as fair as any place for it, and desires you to acquaint Dr. Woodroffe of this, and that unless he may compleat the business he will be wholly off, and will print a vindication of the whole affair."

A month later Sir Thomas writes again that he had been "so tricked and boggled with at Oxford that he is resolved, if they do not let him settle at Gloucester Hall in a short time, he will be wholly off." Again, in October, the Master of Balliol was warned to return from Bristol to Oxford if he wished to protect the interests of his College. Apparently the Master was not ashamed to assert that Balliol was so closely connected with Worcestershire that "it was commonly known as Worcester College." The Balliol interest reached its culminating point in December, 1699, when Sir Thomas gave Dr. Baron a copy of Dr. Woodroffe's statutes, with instructions to alter them so as to meet the case of Balliol.

Then there was an entirely new scheme. Sir Thomas Cookes persuaded the grand juries of Worcestershire to present him with a memorial requesting him to transfer his benefaction to that county, and to erect workhouses. This they accordingly did, and the coquetry with Balliol was brought to an end. From this point the parties concerned lost all patience with this most dilatory of founders. Dr. Woodroffe went about giving vent to pointed references to the fate of Ananias and Sapphira, and Dr. Baron abandoned all faith in the resolution or good faith of the benefactor. Amid all this confusion Sir Thomas suddenly veered round to Gloucester Hall. Then he submitted a case to a noble lord, asking him whether he was bound in any way to Gloucester Hall.

Before a reply had been received, he had come back to Balliol again.

"I do solemnly declare" (he wrote) "if I were once assured, under his Lordship's hand, that I might with a safety and prudence retreat from Gloucester Hall, I would immediately settle my charity at Balliol College."

The noble lord's answer arrived on March 28, 1700. He said that he could not tell "what vows to God or promises to men, or personal resolutions," Sir Thomas had made, but he was under no legal obligation. Sir Thomas at once asserted that his conscience was not bound if he was not bound in law, and forthwith reverted to the workhouses.

By this time the Duke of Ormonde had given his consent to the change by which Sir Thomas was to become Patron of the new College, on condition that the Chancellor should be allowed to nominate two of the scholars, and Dr. Woodroffe came down to Feckenham to see Sir Thomas on the matter; but Sir Thomas, "who could not possibly be easy under all this teasing, refused to see him," and Dr. Woodroffe had to shoot his shaft from the Feckenham pulpit on May 23 on the occasion of the charity sermon. Like Dr. Baron, he insisted that men of ability should do good while they live; and Dr. Baron, who must have had a very short memory, professed to be aghast at the indelicacy of the insinuation. George Hickes, who claimed to be a connoisseur in such matters, wrote in reference to this sermon:

"I have read much flattery in my time, especially in French dedications; but so false, so fulsome, flattery was

FOUNDATION OF WORCESTER COLLEGE 167

never written as in that dedication to Sir Thomas Cookes. All men who know Sir Thomas will think it a most accomplished piece of its kind."

At any rate, the sermon accomplished its object, and for the next few months Sir Thomas was in favour of the Hall, employing a counsel to examine its title. Dr. Woodroffe, during 1701, dined with Sir Thomas. In one of his pamphlets he gave a wrong date to the dinner, and Dr. Baron thought it a very pretty piece of raillery to point out that at the date in question Sir Thomas was giving the worms a dinner. A difficulty as to title followed, and in April, 1701, the grand jury were persuaded to send in another address; and now it almost seemed as if the question involved a race against death. Sir Thomas said that if the consent of the Bishop of Worcester could be obtained, the money should go according to the address. At exactly the same time he wrote to Dr. Woodroffe that he "disowned the project of the gentlemen at the Assizes," and Dr. Woodroffe made a last desperate effort to persuade Sir Thomas to reduce his will to some more definite shape. Meanwhile, four gentlemen of Worcestershire were riding up to London to get the Bishop's consent to the change. They interviewed the Bishop in the Lobby of the House of Lords, and he said that he would give his answer as soon as he returned to the country. The Bishop returned a fortnight later, only to find that Sir Thomas had died on June 8, 1701, at the age of fifty-two.

"I shall leave" (says Dr. Baron) "the world to judge of the decency of the underhand proceedings of Sir Thomas towards my Lords the Bishops, as well as the insincerity of the practice itself, being too notorious and evident to need any explanation, and too gross to be capable of an excuse."

By the terms of his will he was locked into his vault at Tardebigg, which was "firmly made up with screws, bars, and other irons and engines." But these precautions did not save his tomb from desecration. By his own directions he was buried with a gold chain and locket round his neck, and two diamond rings of no great value on his fingers. About the year 1750 David Cookes, Esq., heir of the family, came with a hook and a pair of tongs, and searching, found the things above mentioned. He left no children, his nearest relative at the time of his death being Mercie, who married Henry Winford; but this branch of the family became extinct in the male line. However, Henry Cookes, the uncle of Sir Thomas Cookes, had eight children, the eldest of whom, John, had fourteen children. John's youngest son, Henry, had a son Thomas, who had eight children, and several of the name of Cookes, who are descended from this branch of the family, have claimed the privileges of Founder's kin at the College almost up to the present generation. The last Founder's kin Fellow is still alive. Another connection, though a distant one, of Sir Thomas was William Chetle, a benefactor to the College. In the female line the Founder has had kin at the College in the person of Samuel Foote, and a long succession of Amphletts, who still flourish within the College.

If the death of Sir Thomas removed the chief obstacle to the foundation of Worcester College, it created a

FOUNDATION OF WORCESTER COLLEGE 169

new one in the shape of a will which was proved on October 15, 1701, in the Prerogative Court of Canterbury. It was dated February 19, 1696, so it was clear that the eloquence of Dr. Baron, of Dr. Woodroffe, and of all the grand juries of Worcestershire, had been totally ineffectual. He thereby devised to the Archbishop of Canterbury, the Bishops of Worcester, Oxford, Lichfield, and Gloucester, and to the Vice-Chancellor and all the heads of the Colleges and Halls in Oxford, the sum of £10,000, to be paid within eighteen months next after his decease, to be by them, or the major part of them, laid out and disposed of upon trust that they should either erect and build upon an ornamental pile of building in Oxford, and thereto add, raise, create, or endow such and so many scholars, places, and Fellowships as they should think the £10,000 and lands therewith purchased would support, or else that they should add to or endow such other College or Hall in Oxford with such and so many Fellowships and scholar places as they should think most fit and convenient. And he constituted the Bishops of Worcester and Oxford, and the Vice-Chancellor of Oxford, to be visitors of the said foundations. Then follows a clause giving preference to Founder's kin, and to boys bred in his schools of Bromsgrove and Feckenham; in default of such boys, there was to be a preference for boys bred in the free schools of Worcester, Hartlebury, and Kidderminster.

The prospects of Gloucester Hall under this will must have seemed more remote than ever. Not only was the government of the charity vested for the most part in a body of men who were of all others least likely to favour Dr. Woodroffe's claims, but there were phrases in the will itself which plainly seemed to exclude Gloucester Hall. Critics pointed with glee to the words " an ornamental pile of building," and asked Dr. Woodroffe how he could apply such a phrase to Gloucester Hall, which he himself had declared in the patent of 1698 to be little better than a ruin, and, moreover, as Dr. Baron declared, in the very uttermost skirts of the suburbs of the city, and, which is worst, in a most notoriously vicious and scandalous neighbourhood : " Prorsus desolata jacuit unde retro omnia fluere subrui pæne totius aulæ fundamenta nec quicquam nisi moles ædificiorum inanes deploranda rudera et meros ruinarum cumulos ubique conspici."

Dr. Woodroffe apparently thought that his best course was to try and push the matter through as quickly as possible before other claimants appeared. With this object in view he went to the House of Lords. On February 5, 1702, a committee was appointed to prepare a Bill to carry Sir Thomas's charity into effect. It consisted of four dukes, one marquis, twenty-one earls, the Archbishop of Canterbury, and ten bishops and thirty-three barons. Between March 30 and April 13 it passed through all the necessary stages to third reading in the House of Lords. On the last of these days it was sent down from the Lords to the House of Commons, and Dr. Woodroffe prepared and circulated his case of Gloucester Hall among the members. On April 20 the second reading was passed, but the motion to commit it was rejected on April 29 by a majority of 16 (27 to 43).

The reason of the failure was fairly obvious. Dr. Woodroffe, in preparing the Bill, had entirely neglected

FOUNDATION OF WORCESTER COLLEGE 171

the terms of the will, and had attempted to carry the patent of 1698, together with the statutes contained in that patent. The Bill disregarded the trustees appointed by the will, and Sir Thomas Winford was introduced into the scheme, though the will had not mentioned him.

The difficulties of title were to be obviated by a clause which compelled St. John's College to renew the lease of the College for ever at a rent of £5 10s., and even if St. John's College were willing to do this, it was clearly not fair to bind their successors by such a clause. Dr. Woodroffe says it was rejected in a thin house and in a hurry of business, but the majority against it was decisive. The Doctor now published

"a letter from a member of the House of Commons in answer to a letter from a member of the University inquiring how the Bill for settling Sir Thomas Cookes' charity of £10,000 for the erecting and endowing of Worcester College came to be rejected in their House."

He seems to have had thoughts of applying a second time to Parliament. Shortly afterwards Dr. Baron,* who had by this time given up all thought of securing the endowment for Balliol, published his "Case of Gloucester Hall in Oxford, rectifying the false stating thereof by Benjamin Woodroffe." It has been the source from which the account of these transactions has for the most part been drawn. From the date of this pamphlet the process of the negotiations becomes

* The tradition that Dr. Baron was the author of "The Case of Gloucester Hall" is almost as old as the pamphlet itself. As we do not know on what the tradition is based, we have assumed its truth; but the internal and external evidence make it difficult to believe he wrote the pamphlet.

obscure. St. Edmund Hall and Magdalen Hall were both competitors for the prize. How nearly the money went to the latter of these institutions may be judged from a passage in Parker's " Ephemeris." The " Ephemeris" is one of those Oxford almanacs which flourished in the eighteenth century, and gave grossly incorrect accounts of the various foundations in Oxford. Under the heading " Worcester College" it says :

" First built by William of Wainfleete, the founder of Magdalen College, and called it Magdalen Hall, as adjoining and belonging to it. Since in the year 1708, being the seventh year of Queen Anne, Sir Thomas Cook, in the county of Worcester, by his last will became a worthy benefactor, from whence it is called Worcester College, but the number of students is not as yet determined or compleatly fixed."

It appears that nineteen of the thirty trustees met on November 22, 1707, and sixteen of them were in favour of settling the charity at Magdalen Hall. Of the remaining trustees, three were against the scheme and eleven did not act. The most influential supporters of the Worcester College scheme were the Archbishop of Canterbury and the Bishops of Worcester and Oxford, who were trustees, and Winford, who was not a trustee; while the Oxford trustees were unfavourable to Gloucester Hall, doubtless owing to their hostility to Dr. Woodroffe. No doubt it was by their instigation that an information in Chancery, which had been dormant since 1702, was revived in the following year. Dr. Woodroffe published a circular letter, complaining "again, according to his usual veracity, of Dr. Manders getting hands to pervert the

FOUNDATION OF WORCESTER COLLEGE 173

charity, and challenging all opponents to answer therein at law." Four years later the matter was before the Lord Chief Justice, who was trying to gather particulars of Dr. Woodroffe's sermon at the burial of Sir Thomas. A few days later a fear was expressed that Dr. Woodroffe would find means of tampering with the witnesses in the case, and in September of that year matters seem to have arrived at a deadlock; for the Bishop of London wrote to the Master of University, entreating him to consult a little with Mr. Vice-Chancellor about Sir Thomas Cookes' bounty.

"There are some that intend if they can to defeat the charity, and others are so stiff to their own inclinations that makes it almost as unhappy on their side. If therefore you do not agree upon some place in the University without the necessity of preferring this or that place to another, and resolve to be unanimous in resigning up your private inclinations to a common consent, it may quickly be too late to repent you had not so done. This between you and me."

No doubt, too, Oxford was beginning to look askance at Dr. Woodroffe. He was no longer the successful Canon of Christchurch, whom a turn of the wheel had made Dean, and might make Dean again. The total failure of the Greek College must have weakened his prestige in the University, and the high hopes with which he had entered on the Principality of Gloucester Hall had for the most part been wrecked. Oxford always had an object-lesson before their eyes in the shape of "Woodroffe's Folly." Moreover, he had made a second marriage, which had involved him in the greatest pecuniary difficulties, if it did not cover him with ridicule. His second wife was Mary, one of the three sisters and co-heiresses of William and Richard Marbury, of Marbury, in Cheshire, a country gentleman possessing heavily encumbered estates. Some time previous to 1705 the property had come to the sisters. The estate came into Chancery on the petition of the mortgagees and bond-debtors, and Dr. Woodroffe, in right of his wife, seems to have acted with his usual exaggerated hopefulness. He made a bid for the estates on behalf of the three sisters of £19,000. Unfortunately, when the time came for completing the contract, Dr. Woodroffe either would not or could not pay the money. Another sale had to take place, and again Dr. Woodroffe bid £19,000, and put down £2,000 as earnest money. But the creditors and other parties interested were unwilling to suffer in the same way a second time. They moved that the bid should be disallowed, and, contrary to all conceivable rules of equity, Earl Rivers was allowed to make an equal bid in open court. Though Dr. Woodroffe protested that his original bid stood good, and that, if necessary, he was willing to outbid Earl Rivers, the Master of the Rolls adjudged Earl Rivers the highest bidder.

Two lawsuits followed, both of which were taken up to the House of Lords, and in both Dr. Woodroffe was defeated. It is easy to see how this must have crippled the Doctor. The estate was sold at far below its proper value, the bondholders and mortgagees, who had the first claim, were paid in full; nothing was left over for Dr. Woodroffe, and he had no balance to meet his previous outlay. Thus in 1711 we hear that the small rent of £5 10s. per annum payable to St. John's

FOUNDATION OF WORCESTER COLLEGE 175

College by Gloucester Hall was no less than seven years in arrear. Under the circumstances, it is not surprising that he very soon found himself in the Fleet, a fate which was probably unique for an ex-Dean of Christchurch, though it has been the lot of many better men.

It is not clear how long the animosity of his creditors kept him there, but the next assault was made on his Canonry at Christchurch.

On April 16, 1709, it became known in Oxford that his creditors were making an attempt to sequestrate his Canonry for a debt of £839, but Dr. Stratford, the Treasurer of Christchurch, refused to pay the money. For his refusal to pay he was prosecuted in the Vice-Chancellor's Court. But Christchurch was by charter exempt from the jurisdiction of this Court, and the only result was the annoyance of " old smooth-boots," as Hearne loved to call " that old hypocritical, ambitions, drunken sot, William Lancaster," Vice-Chancellor of Oxford and Provost of Queen's.

All these troubles were enough to break the spirit of any man, and it was probably to them that Dr. Woodroffe succumbed. He died on August 14, 1711. The bell rang out at Christchurch at two in the afternoon.

" He was a learned man " (says Hearne), "that is, so far as related to the languages, being well skilled in Greek and Latin and some of the Orientals, and would write very handsomely, and speak very neatly off-hand in Latin, but wanted judgment very much, and was, moreover, of a strange, unsettled, whimsical temper, which brought him into debt."

There was apparently some little difficulty in finding a successor to Dr. Woodroffe. The post of Principal of Gloucester Hall, even with a Provostry in prospect, must have been exceedingly unpromising. The first offer was made to Dr. Hudson, librarian of the Bodleian (the librarian who wished to throw away the copy of Milton's poems, presented by the author in 1647). He became Principal of St. Mary Hall in 1711. On his refusal, the office was offered to, and accepted by, Dr. Richard Blechynden, a Fellow of St. John's, and thus the old connection between the two colleges was restored. The new Principal was forty-three years of age. He had matriculated at St. John's College in 1685. He was a Doctor of Civil Law, and had held in succession the livings of Codford St. Mary, Wilts, and Kingston Bagpuze, Berks, both in the gift of St. John's College. In 1710 he became Canon of Rochester, and in 1711 Canon of Gloucester. In 1714 he was presented to the living of Nuneham Courtney, which had formerly been held by his predecessor, Dr. Byrom Eaton.

With Dr. Woodroffe's death, all the difficulties that had beset the foundation of Worcester College appear to have vanished. What was denied to Dr. Woodroffe, the Whig and the scholar, was readily granted to Richard Blechynden, a man after Oxford's own heart, " good," as Hearne tells us, " for nothing but drinking and keeping jolly company." No doubt matters were facilitated by the fact that the new Principal was a member of the foundation of the College which possessed the freehold of the Hall. It is not known when the matter was finally settled, but it was a considerable

FOUNDATION OF WORCESTER COLLEGE 177

time after 1711. Among other evidence of the suitability of Gloucester Hall for the charity was a report to the effect that "Gloucester Hall buildings and quadrangles and gardens are three times as much as Magdalen Hall, and the ground on which ye buildings of Gloucester Hall stand is twice as much as that of Magdalen Hall, and there are large and capacious chambers in Gloucester Hall to receive 20 scholars and 9 are inhabited and ye principall's lodgings are in good repair and fit for a family of 12 persons, and there is a large hall, chapel, buttery, and kitchen, and a large common room lately wainscoated and sash windows, and in laying out about £500 in repairs there will be good conveniences for 60 scholars, and the plaice is pleasantly sttuated and in a good air." In 1713 St. John's consented to alienate the leasehold of the College for a payment of £200 and a quit-rent of 20s. a year. A new body of statutes was drafted, and these, together with the Charter, passed the Great Seal on July 14, only two days before the death of Queen Anne.

The new statutes were very like the old, but the objectionable features were omitted. They open, strangely enough, and rather abruptly, with the clause *De divinis officiis*, which was Section 8 of the 1698 statutes. There are a few changes. Blechynden of St. Jobu's altered the prayers after the "Christchurch" use into prayers after the "St. Johu's" use. Yet both the prayers and the grace were retained to the present generation. The grace has never been abolished. The Bible was to be read during dinner, but the injunction for private reading was omitted. A clause was inserted as to the duties of the Provost, which were " to afford an example of piety, honest conversation, prudence, labour, and study, so that his life might be a mirror to which the whole house should conform." The government of the College was to be in the hands of the Provost and three Senior Fellows, and the register was always signed by three Fellows on this account. The duties of the Vice-Provost remained practically the same, but he was forbidden to expel a member of the College without the Provost's leave. His substitute in absence was to be the Senior Fellow. A new officer was introduced in the person of the Dean, who was to be *censor morum* and president at disputations. Elections to the three offices in the College were to be made annually on St. Andrew's Day.

The clauses providing for the appointment of the Provost, Fellows and scholars were repeated almost verbally, but a few alterations were made. The question of patronage, which for sixteen years had been the chief obstacle to the foundation of the College, was settled in accordance with the original plan by making the Chancellor patron of the College. Founder's kin were excluded from their right of becoming Fellows after two years as scholars. Kidderminster was added to Worcester and Hartlebury as the schools from which scholars might be chosen; and no Fellow was to have property of his own of more than double the value of his Fellowship, or hold a living rated at more than £10 per annum in the King's Books. Scholars were to be elected on St. John the Baptist's Day. New clauses were added *De absentia* and *De cameris*. Dinner in Hall was made compulsory by the statute *De mensis*. The clause *De exercitiis* provided for an arduous series of disputations in the public hall.

On all public occasions and in Hall Latin was to be the language employed, though an exception was made in favour of College meetings. The Provost was to receive £80 a year, the six Fellows were to receive £30 a year apiece, and the scholars £13 6s. 8d. The Fellows and scholars were also to receive fourpence a day for commons, and twopence a day for drink and bread. The Vice-Provost, the Dean, and the Bursar were to receive £5 a year each, and the Chaplain £10 a year. The steward or seneschal was to receive £5 a year. There were to be four college servants, the promus, coquus, janitor and tonsor. The two first were to receive £5 a year, the janitor £8 a year, and the tonsor, who lingered as a college official almost to the present day, 20s. Bachelors were to give a dinner on taking their degree, or pay 20s. to the Provost, and Masters of Arts were not to spend more than 40s. over the public dinner they gave on taking this degree. The College gates were to be closed before ten o'clock, and the keys given to the Provost. Particular directions were given as to an "ostiolum" on the south-east part of the College. The Provost, Bursar and one of the Senior Fellows were to visit the College estates annually, or at least once in seven years. If ever the revenues of the College went down, *quod avertat Deus*, the salaries of all the officials were to be curtailed; but any advantage that came of an increase in revenue was to go to the common chest. The register was to be kept in the Bursar's room, but the Provost might take it to his lodgings at his pleasure. There were to be two iron chests, which were to be kept in a convenient place. One was to contain muniments, the other was to contain money and the rarer of the College silver and plate. There were to be three keys, which were to be and are still kept by the Provost, Bursar and Dean respectively. Two copies of the statutes were to be made: one copy was to be kept chained in the library, so that all who were interested in them might read; the other was to be in the possession of the Provost. They were to be publicly read, at least once a year, by the Provost or Vice-Provost. This was done till 1856, when the new ordinances came into operation. The Latin prayers were dropped at the same time, and the copies used in chapel distributed among the members of the College.

The Bishops of Oxford and Worcester and the Vice-Chancellor of Oxford were appointed visitors.

Fifteen days after the passing of the statutes the Provost and the first six Fellows were admitted, and so, after a rather precarious existence of a hundred and sixty-four years, Gloucester Hall ceased to exist as a Hall.

But the breach of continuity was of the slightest character. Discussions as to the antiquity of an institution are singularly profitless, but it may be pointed out that there is only one serious break in the history of the College since the thirteenth century, and that was for the brief period when Gloucester Hall was occupied as a Bishop's palace. The change that Gloucester Hall underwent in 1714 was not nearly so considerable as that which New College, for instance, underwent when it opened its doors to a large under-

FOUNDATION OF WORCESTER COLLEGE 181

graduate population, or that which a school like St. Paul's or Christ's Hospital undergoes when it is torn up by its roots and transplanted into a new country. It is no more reasonable to calculate the date of Worcester College from the date when it changed its name than to date a lady's age from the time when she undergoes a similar metamorphosis. That the College at the same time received a settlement of £15,000* makes no more difference in the one case than the other. The College retained the books, the silver, and the buildings of the Hall. The Provost of the College had been Principal of the Hall. The whole body of the commoners and one of the Fellows, Roger Bourchier, passed straight from the Hall to the College.

* The original sum had been increased by the accumulated interest of twelve years.

CHAPTER IX

WORCESTER COLLEGE IN THE EIGHTEENTH AND NINE-TEENTH CENTURIES

WITH the record of the foundation of Worcester College the picturesque and striking episodes of its history come to an end. Its life during the past 180 years has been as uneventful as its early history was varied and stormy. It has suffered no great or radical change in its statutes. It has had no Provost round whose name has gathered a great body of tradition. The fluctuations in the price of wheat have marked the most important changes in its position, and a succession of Fellows have come and gone like the birds in some immemorial rookery, as an Oxford writer has aptly put it, doing their good work in their generation, and then passing out of the knowledge and the memory of the University in which they once no doubt played an adequate part. Of successive Provosts of the College Dr. Blechynden is a name and not even a memory. Dr. Gower passed sixty-two years on the foundation of the College, but his name is mainly kept alive by the stormy three years during which Samuel Foote disturbed his tranquillity, and by numerous books in the library which bear his name as donor. The name of Sheffield, his successor, scratched in some idle moment on a pane of glass in the Provost's lodgings, has proved the most lasting memorial of a Provostship which extended through six academic generations, while the name of Dean Landon mainly survives as the accidental host of the allied Sovereigns on the occasion of their memorable visit in 1814.

But though the life of the College has been even, it has not been torpid. The years have brought the College a series of benefactions which have added materially to its originally scanty endowments, have restored and rebuilt, and in some cases embellished its buildings, and have given it an increased dignity and status in the University.

We deal in the next chapter with the endowments of the College and various other matters which deserve special notice. In the present chapter we may group together such miscellaneous facts as serve to make up the history of the College.

Perhaps the most important task which the new College had to face was the acquisition of its freehold. Originally it possessed not an acre of land in Oxford, and even its site was a leasehold held of St. John's College. The first considerable benefaction to the landed property of the College was the purchase of the whole of the garden on the south of the College, together with the tenements and appurtenances thereto belonging. £850 was paid for the purchase, which must have extended to Hythe bridge and included Worcester House. In 1743 the alienation money due to St. John's College was paid, and the receipt for £200 put into the chest. In 1744 the College purchased from St. John's the garden and meadow to the north and west of the College, together with the house called the Cock and Bottle. The purchase would probably include the brewhouse which still stands, though about the year 1870 the College ceased to brew its own ale. In 1801 the College bought for £1,330 the King's Head opposite to the front of the College, and in 1813 the lease of the premises on the east front of the College was bought for £1,200. At the same time the Fellows' garden was established, and it was decided that two small meadows on the west of the Provost's lodgings should be kept for the use of the Provost. In 1820 Beaumont Street was commenced, and an exchange of property followed. The laying out of Beaumont Street had been in contemplation for many years, and by the Act of 1775 dealing with the Eaton property, which will be presently referred to, the College obtained power to purchase lands on the site of Beaumont Street and to convert them into a highway. In 1823 the College built three new houses in Beaumont Street, and granted a lease of them for forty years. In 1832 another house was built at the bottom of Beaumont Street. Meanwhile premises had been acquired at the top of the same street on the north side, and in 1838 the Black Boy in St. Giles's, together with other premises, was added to them at a cost of £2,000. Two years later the Taylorian galleries were built, and the College sold the whole block of buildings to the University for £4,472. In the year 1878 began that fall of rents which has lowered the revenues of the College to a point probably below that of any other in Oxford.

The growth of the buildings kept pace with the growth of the property. We refer elswehere to the chapel, hall, and library, and to the buildings on the north side of the College. The easternmost of these chambers were built out of Dr. Clarke's funds in 1753, and the work was completed and the Provost's lodgings erected prior to 1773. In December, 1821, three new sets of rooms, together with servants' offices, were fitted up in the "space afforded by the old College chapel." But we have no means of saying where these rooms were. In October, 1822, it was ordered that all rooms capable of holding undergraduates should be fitted up, and in December, 1824, it was resolved to raise the roof of a part of the old building, in order to obtain six additional sets of rooms at a cost of £800. On January 11, 1844, it was resolved to build a new kitchen and buttery, together with other offices and out-houses, and to commute the present kitchen (that on No. 12 staircase) into rooms, and to erect four new sets of rooms over a portion of the old offices. Lastly, in 1865 it was proposed to fit up the rooms over the hall for the reception of undergraduates. This was a scheme of Dr. Cotton for meeting the demand for University extension. It was necessary at that time for undergraduates to reside in college till the completion of their third year, and every corner of the college was consequently utilized. But the idea was absolutely impracticable. The rooms would have been dungeons, and the locality has since been fitted up for the uses of the library.

Of successive Provosts of the College, we may doubt whether Dr. Richard Blechynden was the sot represented by Hearne, for he was on intimate terms with Dr. George Clarke. He kept the College books with some care, but that is the extent of our knowledge of his twenty-two years' reign. He held the living of Fairford, in Gloucestershire, and died on October 17, 1736.

His successor was William Gower, who was appointed Provost by the Earl of Arran within seven days of Blechynden's death. He had been one of the first scholars elected to the College, and remained on the books for a term of sixty-three years. He was presented to the living of Whitfield, in Northamptonshire, which was for many years held by successive Provosts of Worcester College.

Of his personal character it does not seem possible to speak with any certainty. The author of "Oxford in the Last Century," himself a Worcester man, describes him as "the most lumbering of pedants," while Dr. King says that he was acquainted

"with three persons only who spoke English with that eloquence and propriety that if all they said had been immediately committed to writing, any judge of the English language would have pronounced it an excellent and beautiful style."

The three persons thus referred to are Dr. Gower, Bishop Atterbury, and Dr. Johnson.

But it must be confessed that the chief interest is given to Dr. Gower's reign by an event which could hardly bring him credit. On June 8, 1737, Samuel Foote, of Worcester School, put in his claim to be elected to a scholarship as founder's kin. Samuel

Foote's great-grandfather, Sir Edward Dingley, was father of the mother of Sir Thomas Cookes. On this rather slender basis of relationship Henry Brookes, Barrister-at-law of Oxford, came to the conclusion that Samuel Foote was both *cognatus* and *consanguineus* to the founder, and he was accordingly elected. But he was too reckless and disorderly to be tolerated even in that age of academic disorder. He used to act Punch through the streets of Oxford, and amuse the crowd with his ridicule of the pomposity of the Provost, who was the object of his especial persecution. On one occasion, when summoned to receive a reprimand from the insulted dignitary, he presented himself with the greatest appearance of gravity and submission, but with a dictionary under his arm. No sooner had the pompous harangue begun than at the first long word " Foote interrupts the doctor, begs pardon with great formality, and turns over the dictionary to find out its meaning, and after a moment's pause requests the Provost to proceed." But this did not end his career, which reached a climax when he dashed through Oxford in a coach-and-six, tricked out in ridiculous finery and attended by a couple of footmen, not to mention a companion quite unrecognised by the College authorities. On February 25, 1740, he was formally deprived of his scholarship. The entry is in the College register:

"Whereas Samuel Foote, Scholar of Worcester College, by a long course of ill-behaviour has rendered himself obnoxious to frequent censures of the society publick and private, and having whilst he was under censure for lying out of College insolently and presumptuously withdrawn himself and refused to answer to several heinous crimes objected to him, though duly cited by the Provost by an instrument in form, in not appearing to the said citation for the above-mentioned reasons, his scholarship is declared void, and he is hereby deprived of all benefit and advantage of his said scholarship."

This resolution is signed by three of the College authorities.

There seems to be good reason to believe that Dr. Gower was neither a capable nor a popular head of the College. The building both of chapel and hall stagnated during his reign. The junior members of the society seem to have been exceptionally disorderly, and his gross violations of the statutes at last brought him to an open rupture with the Fellows.

The year 1760 seems to have been a time of considerable disturbance. One of the scholars was publicly admonished; "the clause of the statute of disobedience was read to him," and it was declared that upon his next offence he should be removed without delay. The next offence occurred within a space of five months, but he was partially forgiven, though he was gated for two months and condemned to translate Tully, "De Officiis." Another scholar of the same year was postponed from his degree for "an idle and disorderly life," and at a later date he was ordered to repeat a declamation in chapel on Saturday, May 23, and therein ask pardon of the Senior Fellow and the society for past offences. A third scholar was suspended for six months for not performing a task, and a year later he was deprived of his scholarship for indecent behaviour in chapel.

William Gower, who died July 19, 1777, during his last years appears to have been in conflict with William Sheffield, the Vice-Provost. All the College books come to a complete standstill as soon as Dr. Sheffield was appointed Provost, but this did not prevent him from criticising the action of his predecessors in the books which were handed over to him. As to several elections made by Provost Gower in his last years, he adds a note that they were either unstatutable or contrary to the usage of the College. He also expresses some impatience with the late Provost's handwriting, and against some of the less legible entries he adds an explanatory note.

Matters reached a crisis in 1775, and though the dispute that followed is intrinsically uninteresting, we may be pardoned if we refer to it rather fully on account of the picture of academic life it gives us in days when Worcester College was more closely united to Worcestershire.

On Monday, July 5, the Vice-Provost was summoned by the Provost to attend the election of a Fellow on the Cookes' foundation. When he came to the Provost's room he found two Fellows on Mrs. Eaton's foundation and one upon Dr. Clarke's foundation there. He protested against their presence at the election, as only a Cookes' Fellow was entitled to elect to the Cookes' Fellowship. But his protest was disregarded, and a Fellow was elected and admitted. In the afternoon the Provost and Hugh Morgan, a Bachelor on Mrs. Eaton's foundation, set out for Worcestershire to elect two scholars, and Mr. Sheffield set out at eleven o'clock the same evening, and arrived at Worcester early on Wednesday morning, when he summoned all the old foundation Fellows to meet him at the Bell in the Broad Street, which they did accordingly. A protest against the proceedings was made out and served upon the Provost and Mr. Hugh Morgan at the Hoppole Inn the same evening. The Provost took no heed of this, and proceeded to Hartlebury, where he elected Edward Waldron scholar upon the old foundation. The result of these irregular proceedings was an appeal to the visitor, who supported the contention of Dr. Sheffield, and the elections made by Dr. Gower were declared null and void. An additional interest is given to the occasion by the fact that one of the scholars illegally rejected by Dr. Gower was Whittington Landon, who lived to be Provost. Thus Whittington Landon forms the connecting-link between Gower, who was one of the first scholars of Worcester College, and Dr. Cotton, who was Provost till 1880, and almost belongs to the present generation. This practice of going down in person into Worcestershire to elect scholars for Worcester College was continued till near the close of Dr. Cotton's Provostship.

On Dr. Sheffield's death in 1795 Dr. Whittington Landon was appointed his successor. He was a handsome and burly man, but in his later years he was afflicted with gout, which made him lame. He was appointed Keeper of the Archives in 1796, and became Vice-Chancellor of the University in 1802. After holding a number of livings he was appointed to the Deanery of Exeter in 1813. For such a dignitary the path from Worcester College in those days before the opening of Beaumont Street must have been beset with

From a photograph by the]   *[Oxford Camera Club*

INTERIOR OF THE CHAPEL

Plate VII

difficulties. Preceded by his bedels with their gold and silver maces, he would walk

"through Gloucester Green, then the acknowledged site of the pig market, and down the whole length of Friars Entry, at the risk of being besprinkled by trundled mops in those straits of Thermopylæ, of stumbling over buckets, knocking over children, of catching the rinsings of basins, and ducking under linen lines suspended across from the opposite houses."

It is certainly a tribute to his deportment that in spite of these disadvantages he earned the nickname of Old Glory. Owing to the illness of the Vice-Chancellor he was the host of the allied Sovereigns on the occasion of their visit to Oxford in June, 1814. One pleasant trait is recorded of his relations with the College. Owing to the gout he used to be brought to chapel every Sunday morning in a Bath chair. The Fellows present always attended him back to his lodgings, a practice retained to the present day. Another episode renders his Provostship notable. In 1809 F. H. Brickenden was the first member of Worcester College to be appointed proctor. Worcester College was not then, nor till 1863, on the proctorial rota, but proctors were occasionally nominated from its ranks by other colleges. Brickenden was somewhat more severe than discreet, and in the event an action was brought against him by one Williams

"for depositing the plaintiff in the castle for one night, and for marching him through the streets next morning to the Vice-Chancellor's justice room without suffering him to lay aside the dress of a mail coach guard in which he was found."

Since that date Worcester College has had two proctors, John Moore and James Hannay, before it was admitted to the proctorial rota, and five since.

As Dr. Gower will be remembered by Samuel Foote, Dr. Whittington Landon will be remembered by Thomas de Quincey, the most illustrious member of the College in his day. He remained on the College books from 1803 to 1816. There are various accounts of his career at the College.

"I neglected" (says he) "my dress habitually, and wore my clothes till they were threadbare, partly under the belief that my gown would conceal defects, more from indisposition to bestow on a tailor what I had destined for a bookseller. At length, however, an official person sent me a message on the subject. This, however, was disregarded, and one day I discovered that I had no waistcoat that was not torn or otherwise dilapidated, whereupon buttoning my coat to the throat and drawing my gown close about me, I went into the hall."

His companions asked him whether he had seen the latest *Gazette*, which was said to contain an Order in Council interdicting the use of waistcoats, and they expressed a hope that so sensible an order would be followed by one interdicting the use of breeches, which are still more disagreeable to pay for.

But even at Oxford he appears to have impressed his teachers with an idea of his extraordinary abilities. Dr. Goodenough, one of his examiners, said he was the cleverest man he had ever met with, and he would undoubtedly have taken high honours in the examination had he not disappeared from Oxford the day before the *vivâ voce*.

On the death of Dr. Landon on December 29, 1838, Dr. Robert Lynch Cotton was appointed Provost. He had been elected from Charterhouse to a Holford exhibition at the College in 1812. He became a Clarke scholar in 1815, and was a pupil of Thomas Arnold. He was reading with him when the news came of Arnold's election at Oriel. In 1816 he was elected Fellow, and served the offices of Tutor, Bursar and Dean. In 1823 he became Vicar of Denchworth, a College living which he served from Oxford, still remaining tutor. Stories illustrative of the simplicity of his character and the goodness of his heart still survive. To secure his two servants should not starve, he ordered the butcher to supply a leg of mutton every day, and a friend who once accompanied him was startled to be set down to a mid-day meal of four steaming legs of mutton, the accumulations of the week served in his honour. Bishop Wilberforce, visiting him at his Vicarage, was puzzled by a cupboard full of linen, all marked " W. S." This he found was prepared in readiness for " wet strangers." Dean Burgon, himself an old alumnus of the College, tells how

> " 'Twas sport to see
> When beggars chased him near the College wall
> (Some mother of a fabulous brood of bairns),
> How soon he'd strike his colours to the foe !
> Ever the first in chapel—at his prayers
> A homily to inattentive hearts—
> I think the College loved him to a man."

For Dean Burgon's sketch of Dr. Cotton as " the humble Christian," the reader may consult his " Lives of Twelve Good Men." In 1838 he was appointed Provost of the College by the Duke of Wellington, the old comrade in arms of Lord Combermere, Dr. Cotton's relative. An interesting fact in connection with the Great Duke may be recorded. One of the last books he read—a book which was lying on his table at his death — was the Report of the Oxford University Commission. The copy of the book in question was presented to the Provost by the second Duke in 1853, and by him given to the library of the College. It contains an inscription to the effect that the report was studied by Field Marshal the Duke of Wellington at Walmer Castle on September 13, 1852. Dr. Cotton had been in his day a great rider, though those who knew him in his later days would hardly believe it. In consequence of this characteristic the name of "hard-riding Dick" was conferred upon him by the Rev. John Miller, who had a happy gift in this direction. It was he who suggested the title for the "Christian Year."

Dr. Cotton married a sister of Dr. Pusey, but he himself was always opposed to the Tractarian party. He held the office of Vice-Chancellor of the University from 1852 to 1856, exactly half a century after that office had been held by his predecessor, Dr. Landon. In that capacity he presided over the lunch given by the College on the occasion of Lord Derby's Installation as Chancellor, and dilated at nerveless length upon the greatness of the house of Stanley, while the company were impatiently waiting in vain for speeches from D'Israeli and other famous guests. The Vice-Chancellorship of Dr. Cotton saw the extinction of the Grand Compounder. In 1853 Mr. Baxendale, of Balliol, claimed that if required to pay the higher fees for his Degree he should have the statutory consideration, and the Vice-Chancellor and Proctors were compelled to escort him to the Convocation House, and thence to his College. From that day the University exacted no more Grand Compounder's fees.

There are some reminiscences of the mode of life of the College in Dr. Cotton's days. The tutors, as elsewhere, gave their lectures, or, rather, lessons, consisting of translations by the class with questions and answers, without form or ceremony in their own rooms. After an early dinner they would return to an uncarpeted common room. There after wine long clay pipes were a regular indulgence. An evening walk or other interlude was succeeded by a hot supper at nine, and the evening finished with a rubber. Dr. Cotton in his day was singular in retiring to his rooms after common room without joining the whist and supper party.

The last public appearance of Dr. Cotton was on the occasion of what is believed to be the only infant baptism ever celebrated in the College. He died on December 8, 1880, after a Provostship of forty-one years, and was succeeded by Dr. William Inge, the present Provost, under whom the College has reached perhaps its highest state of efficiency. Dr. Inge was nominated by Lord Salisbury as Chancellor. In future the election is to be made by the Fellows of the College.

One may mention in this place a few names of distinguished members of the College in the present century; the list is entirely confined to deceased members of the College, and the names of distinguished Worcester men who are still alive are omitted.

Among the clergy, Robert James Carr (1792 to 1796) was an intimate friend of the Prince Regent, and as soon as George IV. ascended the throne he was appointed Dean of Hereford. In 1824 he became Bishop of Chichester. He was also Canon of St. Paul's and Clerk to the Closet, an office from which he was dismissed on the accession of the present Queen. In 1831 he was transferred to the Bishopric of Worcester, which he held till his death in 1841. It may have been through his influence that Whittington Landon was appointed to the Deanery of Exeter in 1813. The Garniers, father and son, were two well-known Churchmen and typical Oxford men. Thomas Garnier the elder (1793 to 1796) was Fellow of All Souls, and from 1840 to 1872 Dean of Winchester. He died in 1873 at the age of ninety-eight. His son (1827 to 1830) was, like his father, Fellow of All Souls. In 1859 he became Dean of Ripon, and in 1860 Dean of Lincoln. He died at Lincoln in 1863 as the result of a fall. He was one of the earliest Oxford athletes, and rowed in the University boat-race of 1829. Richard Greswell, if less widely known, was far more closely connected with the College. He will always be remembered by Worcester men as the creator of the College gardens, to which he devoted his bursarial income, and by Churchmen as one of the founders, if not the actual founder, of the National Society. He was one of the founders of the Ashmolean Club and Ashmolean Society, a benefactor of the City in the draining, planting, and improvement of Port Meadow, and the enthusiastic chairman of Mr. Gladstone's Committee in all but his latest contest for the University seat. "His chief characteristics were great and varied learning, boundless benevolence, and a childlike simplicity."

> " To get whose living image see you join
> To childlike guilelessness a sage's wit,
> Truth like a woman's, bounty like a king's."

He was one of the five sons of William Parr Greswell, of Denton, Lancashire, all of whom obtained scholarships and Fellowships at Oxford colleges, and three of them were double first class men.

The intimate friend of Greswell was William Palmer " of Worcester " (as he was designated in distinction to the Rev. William Palmer of Magdalen) who left his mark on the literature of the Church as the author of " Origines Liturgicæ."

Of Colonial Bishops may be mentioned Dr. H. Binney, formerly bursar of the College, Bishop of Nova Scotia, 1851 to 1887; Dr. J. Harding (1861 to 1869), Bishop of Bombay; and Dr. A. W. Poole, Bishop of Japan, 1883 to 1886, while Dr. R. C. Billing was the energetic Bishop Suffragan of Bedford from 1888 to 1895.

Last and not least distinguished of our Churchmen may be mentioned John William Burgon, Dean of Chichester, 1875 to 1888, who brought Worcester College its first Newdigate in 1845, and throughout his life remained a warm and devoted friend of the College.

In science the College has been almost as fortunate as it was in Gloucester Hall days. Andrew Bloxam (1820 to 1827), a member of a family which has been as faithful to Worcester College as it has to Rugby School, was in the words of the " Dictionary of National

Biography" "perhaps the last of the all-round British naturalists," while Robert Bourne (1778), in whose memory a tablet (formerly in the chapel) is now placed on the library staircase, was one of the earliest Oxford Professors of Clinical Medicine. In this place two distinguished political economists and professors of that science at Oxford may be mentioned, namely, J. E. Thorold Rogers and his opponent, Bonamy Price. The former gave the manuscript of his "Dictionary of Aristotle" to Worcester College. The latter, Arnold's favourite pupil, and summoned by him to a Rugby mastership immediately on taking his degree, held the Professorship of Political Economy from 1868 to his death in 1888. In theology the College is represented by the Rev. John Miller, whose Bampton Lectures earned him a great reputation, while in the scholastic profession John Day Collis resuscitated Bromsgrove School, the close connection of which with Worcester College has been already noticed.

In literature we have already referred to Thomas de Quincey. Henry Kingsley was a member of the College from 1850 to 1853. He was an enthusiastic rowing man while at College, and the boat club possesses several memorials of him. He used to occupy the rooms which now form the undergraduates' library.

Two distinguished antiquaries were members of the College, Treadway Russell Nash (1740 to 1757), the historian of Worcestershire, who on his death in 1811 bequeathed a number of valuable pictures to the College, and Thomas Hugo (1839-1842), the great Bewick collector and the historian of the monastic houses of the West of England.

This enumeration may well close with the names of those who have added a lustre to the College as Honorary Fellows, but have been removed by death.

1. Sir Charles T. Newton, the explorer of Halicarnassus, and Keeper of Antiquities at the British Museum.

2. Francis William Newman, the brilliant younger brother of the still more famous Cardinal, logician, Arabic scholar, mathematician, who in his undergraduate days received an honour, which is probably unique, from the examiners in the mathematical school. There are two volumes presented by him to the College library, which bear the following inscription, dated June, 1830:

"The undersigned public examiners, wishing to express their sense of the extensive attainments and superior ability displayed by Francis William Newman at his mathematical examination, May, 1826, request his acceptance of this book ('Mécanique Analytique' of Lagrange) with the 'Système du Monde' of Laplace."

3. Bonamy Price, and (4) Richard Greswell, of whom mention has been already made.

5. Henry Octavius Coxe, "the large-hearted librarian" of Bodley, the eminent palæographer who detected the forgeries of Simonides; "the most generally known and most universally beloved character in Oxford," to quote again Dean Burgon; the most lovable of librarians; the most sympathetic of friends; the most ardent of sportsmen. In his youth he was distinguished as an oarsman, and was chosen for the University eight in 1830, though the race that year fell through. He

entered the Bodleian as sub-librarian in 1838, and was Librarian from 1860 till his death, in 1881. He was the younger brother of Richard, Archdeacon of Lindisfarne, who was also a member of Worcester College.

In 1883 the College celebrated the 600th anniversary of its foundation. Over 100 past and present members were entertained at a banquet in the lately decorated hall. Among the speakers were Professor F. W. Newman, Dean Burgon, and the then representative of the family of the founder of the later College.

CHAPTER X

BENEFACTIONS

It would not be very possible to weave into a continuous historical series an account of the benefactions of which the College has been from time to time the recipient. A list of those which it appears proper to commemorate may best be given in chronological order. But two of these, it may be observed, have a special significance, not only for their magnitude, but still more because they enlarged the original meagre foundation by the incorporation in each case of additional Fellows and scholars, with a corresponding enlargement of the buildings for their accommodation; while in the case of Dr. Clarke, the benefits conferred by him were so numerous and far-reaching as almost to reconstitute the College, and earn for him the title of its second founder. Mrs. Sarah Eaton and Dr. Clarke thus take rank by themselves in the commemoration of our benefactors.

But the modest resources of the original foundation were supplemented from time to time by other benefactions. The first of them was:

1. *The Alcorne Bequest.*—Mrs. Margaret Alcorne, who died on June 16, 1717, bequeathed to the College

one-half of her real and personal estate. After a lengthy litigation, it was decided that she was only tenant for life of her real estate, and consequently one-half of her personal estate only passed to the College. After the payment of legal expenses, this amounted to £798 0s. 3d. It was ordered that this sum should be laid out in buildings, and the chapel, hall, and library were commenced out of the proceeds. The decree was dated June 8, 1720.

2. *The Holford Bequest.*—Lady Elizabeth Holford, of the parish of All Hallows, Steyning, in the city of London, widow of Sir William Holford, in the county of Leicester, founded two exhibitions of the value of £20 per annum each for eight years, and appropriated them to such scholars of Sutton's Hospital (the Charterhouse) as should enjoy the yearly pension allowed by the governors of the same to their scholars.

Her will was dated November 19, 1717, and she gave munificent bequests to no less than four Colleges in the University—namely, Christchurch, Pembroke, Hart Hall, subsequently Hertford, and Worcester. She died in November, 1720.

Hearne gives some interesting particulars of the strange career of this generous benefactress of the University of Oxford:

"Her maiden name was Elizabeth Lewis, being the daughter of one Lewis, a coachman, of Stanton St. John, near Oxford. Being a handsome plump jolly wench, one Mr. Harbin, who belonged to the Custom-House, and was a merchant and very rich, married her, and dying, all he had came to her. For though she had a son by him who was gentleman commoner of Christchurch (and the only child as I have been informed she ever had), yet he died very young to her great grief. After this Sir William Holford married her chiefly for her wealth (her beauty being then much decayed) he being but poor himself, but died before her, and what he had came to his son, Sir William Holford, who dyed not a year agoe being bachellor of arts and Fellow of New College, a rakish drunken sot, and would never acknowledge his mother-in-law, for which she allowed him nothing, and so he dyed poor. The woman dyed very rich in the 70th year or thereabouts of her age, and hath left a vast deal to several charitable uses."

3. *The Finney Bequest.*—James Finney, D.D., Prebendary of Durham, and Rector of Ryton in the county of Durham, left by his will, dated 1727, £2,500 to purchase a freehold estate or estates of the value of £100 a year to found two Fellowships of £40 a year each and two scholarships of £10 a year each. The benefaction was confined in the first place to inhabitants of the moorlands of Staffordshire, and in case of a deficiency in these, to inhabitants of Staffordshire generally, or, in default, to inhabitants of the county of Durham. This bequest found its way into Chancery in the suit of the Attorney-General against Finney, at the relation of the Provost, Fellows, and scholars of Worcester College. But the opposition to the will broke down, and by a decree dated January 25, 1738, the defendant was ordered to pay the costs of the suit, and thus, after eleven years' litigation, the College came by its right.

In process of time the value of the Finney endowment deteriorated to such an extent that Fellows and scholars received a mere pittance, so small that the tradition is the two Fellows would make their annual appearance, consume in kind the emoluments of their Fellowships, and disappear till the next annual occasion. The First Commission consolidated the whole foundation into one scholarship of £60 for natives of Staffordshire, and to facilitate this the last surviving Fellow, the Rev. R. C. Dickerson, resigned his Fellowship in 1866.

4. *The Clarke Bequest.*—By far the most generous benefactor of the College was George Clarke, who may indeed be called its second founder, as the testimony on the loving-cup which he bequeathed to the College records. He was born in 1660, and was the son of Sir William Clarke, who was Secretary at War to the Commonwealth and to Charles II. Brasenose was the first foundation he joined, and in November, 1679, he became Fellow of All Souls, and remained a Fellow of that College for fifty-seven years. He was a man of importance in his day. He was Member for the University in 1685, and again in 1717. In 1721-22 he was re-elected when Dr. King, the Principal of St. Mary Hall, was put up to oppose him, upon which Hearne remarks:

"I heartily wish Dr. King had succeeded, he being an honest man, and very zealous for King James, whereas Clarke is a pitifull, proud sneaker, and an enemy to true loyalty, and was one of those that threw out the bill against occasional conformity in queen Anne's time, and not only so, but canvassed the Court to lay the bill aside, he being then member of parliament for East Lowe, in Cornwall, for which reason he was afterwards put by for that borough."

He held the important offices of Judge Advocate-General, Secretary to the Admiralty, and Secretary to Prince George of Denmark. But his name, in Oxford at least, is held most in remembrance for a series of notable and well-judged benefactions to the Colleges and the University of Oxford. He was a benefactor of Brasenose, of Christchurch, of the Bodleian, and of the University picture-gallery, but he reserved the bulk of his riches for All Souls and Worcester. His connection with Worcester began in his lifetime. Roger Bourchier, whose brother was Principal of Alban Hall, and one of the original executors of his will, was the person through whom he was brought into relation with the College. Almost the first entry in the College register is an account of the dealings of the College with Dr. Clarke. He bound himself to repay sums which Roger Bourchier had advanced for the purpose of restoring the College buildings. His will was made on November 12, 1734, and five successive codicils testify to the growing affection Dr. Clarke felt for the new foundation.

The will embodied the original scheme, which did not suffer any considerable alteration. The sum of £6,000 was to be raised out of his estates, and of that sum £1,000 was to be devoted to the repayment of Mr. Bourchier for the £1,000 he had advanced for building the library, and £3,000 was to be spent on building nine chambers between the library and the Provost's lodgings. £1,000 was given to All Souls, and the balance was to be devoted to the chapel and hall of Worcester College. The new lodgings were to follow the plan given in Williams's "Oxonia Depicta." In addition, he gave the College his estates at Purton and Hill Marton, in the county of Wilts (formerly the seat of the Hyde family and the birthplace of Lord Clarendon), upon trust, first to found six Fellowships of the value of £45 a year, and £25 a year for three scholars; £50 a year was to be devoted to the purchase of books for the library, and £10 a year temporarily for the senior, and £5 a year for the assistant, librarian. There was a further trust to purchase ground on the northwest and south side of the College. Of the various codicils, the second was the most important. Thereby he bequeathed to the College all his books and manuscripts, which were not to be lent out of the library to be used anywhere else on any pretext whatever. This legacy included almost the whole of the collection of Worcester College manuscripts now in the library, and especially the famous Clarke papers, the collection of his father, which are reckoned among the chief authorities on the history of the Civil Wars. This codicil also includes the gift of a magnificent silver grace-cup, weighing 112 oz., which was to be double gilt, unless the testator gilded it in his lifetime. The third codicil empowered the College to spend an additional £5,000 on the new buildings, and to postpone the endowment of the scholarships till the sum was raised. At the same time, the plan given by Williams in "Oxonia Depicta" was to be abandoned, as there was not room in the College for carrying it into execution. The last codicil provided statutes for the library, and added that a preference should be given in the election of scholars to orphans of clergymen of the Church of England.

Dr. Clarke died on October 22, 1736, and was buried in the chapel of All Souls' College.

5. *The Eaton Bequest.*—Mrs. Sarah Eaton, daughter of Dr. Byrom Eaton, formerly Principal of Gloucester Hall, made her last will dated March 18, 1731, and thereby devised her freehold estates at Piddington, in the county of Northampton, and her leasehold estates at Walkeringham, in Northamptonshire, held of Trinity College, Cambridge, and at Fulwell, in Gloucestershire, held of the Dean and Chapter of Gloucester, together with all the residue of her estate, subject to certain annuities, for the purpose of endowing seven Fellowships of £40 a year and five scholarships of £20 a year at Worcester College. The residue was to be divided between the Fellows from time to time, the Provost enjoying double the share of a Fellow. She died on October 1, 1739. The estate amounted to a residue of £5,000, and the real property was worth £123 per annum and the leaseholds £107 per annum. These, together with the Clarke endowments, necessitated a new patent, which was granted on January 18, 1743. The College was thereby empowered to hold £500 per annum real estate, in addition to the £1,500 per annum it was entitled to hold under the patent of 1714, and provision was made for the appointment of thirteen additional Fellows and eight additional scholars.

The bequest created a difficulty, partly because some of the property was leasehold, and partly because there were no chambers in which to lodge the new Eaton scholars and Fellows, since the Provost was by the statutes entitled to the rents and profits of the chambers other than those held by the Cookes Fellows.

Accordingly an Act was obtained in 1745 to obviate the difficulty. The Eaton trustees were empowered to raise £2,533, in order that they might purchase a site for chambers from the Provost and Fellows, and erect chambers thereon. Property of the value of £50 a year was purchased, in order to indemnify the Provost and Fellows for the losses they would incur by admitting Eaton Fellows to office in the College. Of this sum £5 apiece was to be given to the Vice-Provost, Bursar, and Dean respectively, and the residue was to be divided as the College should appoint. In the meanwhile, the profits of the estates were to be accumulated.

Thirty years later, in 1775, it was found necessary again to apply to Parliament for powers to deal with the estate. It had been found that there was not sufficient room to build the new chambers. Consequently the old Provost's lodgings, which lay considerably to the east of the present lodgings, were pulled down, and the present lodgings erected. The buildings had cost about £8,600 in all, and the trustees were retrospectively empowered to spend that amount. The endowment of the Provost, Fellows, and scholars on the Eaton foundation was increased by £5 per annum, and an estate at Lyford was purchased of the value of £400 per annum. The ultimate surplus, after all the purposes of the endowment had been met, was to be divided among the Fellows and scholars on all the foundations. The Bill was opposed in Parliament by John Giles and R. Burd Gabriel, two of the Fellows, on the ground that the Eaton Fellows would have an overwhelming voice in the affairs of the College, and in deference to their wishes it was provided that Eaton Fellows should be elected by the Provost and Fellows on the Cookes foundation, the Eaton scholars should be elected by the Provost and five Senior Fellows, and the Clarke Fellows should be elected by the Provost and Fellows on the foundations of Cookes and Clarke.

It may be noted that this decision was of very nearly the same date as the dispute and the appeal to the Visitor on the subject of the disputed Cookes election. Of course, these quarrels between the different foundations have now become matters of the past. The first scholars and Fellows were elected on June 25, 1773. The endowment was confined to sons of clergymen.

6. *The Chettle Bequest.*—Thomas Chettle, a merchant of the City of London, and brother to Mr. William Chettle, one of the first scholars, and afterwards a Fellow on Sir Thomas Cookes' foundation, by his will dated February 17, 1745, left £1,000 to be divided among the Fellows of the College. But they decided to lay out the sum in the purchase of a property for themselves and their successors. Mr. Chettle was probably one of the founder's kin.

7. *The Gower Bequest.*—Dr. William Gower, the second Provost of the College, who died on July 19, 1777, bequeathed to the College the sum of £3,500 in old South Sea annuities. He also left to the College the reversion of his estate situated at Bramsford, near the city of Worcester, together with a large collection of books for the Library. The Bramsford estate was sold in 1859 for £3,690.

8. *The Kay Bequest.*—In 1787 Mr. Kay left a sum of £15,200 for the endowment of an exhibition of £30 per annum for a native of Yorkshire in the first place,

and for the purchase and improvement of livings. From this fund the following advowsons were purchased:

In 1798 the Rectory of Hoggeston for £1,575.
In 1799 the Rectory of Neen Solars for £2,100.
In 1801 the Rectory of Winford for £1,680.
In 1805 the Rectory of Tadmarton for £810.
In 1819 the Rectory of Dinedor for £1,450.
In 1821 the Rectory of High Ham for £4,200.
In 1862 the Rectory of Blandford St. Mary for £1,937 15s.

9. *The Barnes Scholarship.*—In 1867 Mr. Barnes gave the sum of £3,760 to the College, on condition that the College should pay £120 a year to a scholar, who should be known as the Barnes Scholar. The scholarship was founded to encourage the study of Holy Scripture, and an examination in this subject generally forms part of the competition for the scholarship. The scholarship is open, and is tenable for four years. It was founded in memory of Robert Barnes, who matriculated at the College on October 16, 1861, and died while an undergraduate.

10. *The Cotton Exhibition.*—In November, 1883, a sum of about £500, which had been raised as a memorial to Dr. R. L. Cotton, the late Provost, was received by the College. The proceeds are devoted to an exhibition tenable by a member of the College who is studying theology.

11. *Muckleston Bequest.*—In 1898 the Rev. Rowland Muckleston, formerly Fellow and Tutor, and subsequently Rector of Dinedor, left by his will £2,000 for providing pensions for decayed servants of the College.

BENEFACTIONS

12. *Laycock Bequest.*—In 1899 Mrs. Laycock, to carry out the wishes of her late husband, formerly a member of the College, bequeathed the sum of £5,679 for the endowment of a studentship in Egyptology of an annual value not exceeding £150. Mr. MacIver was elected the first student at Lady Day, 1900.

In addition to the foregoing bequests, there have been several contingent gifts which have failed to take effect.

John Loder, some time of Gloucester Hall, and Vicar of Napton-on-the-Hill, in the county of Warwick, bequeathed his estates at Lechlade and Moreton-in-the-Marsh to the College, subject to certain contingencies. His will was dated in 1742.

By his will, dated April 28, 1750, Chancellor Jones bequeathed £2,000 to the College in certain contingencies which never occurred.

In 1861 the Rev. Benjamin Dent bequeathed £1,000 to certain relatives in succession, and in case of failure to the College, but no failure has occurred.

Minor Gifts.—A number of benefactions will be recorded in connection with the lists of plate and pictures. In addition to these, it may be of interest to enumerate some of the smaller donations received by the College:

In April, 1717, Mr. Edward Dupper, the first Steward of the College, gave the Provost a copy of the Statutes written by himself, and very elegantly bound.

Edward Cooke, of Highnam, near Gloucester, presented five guineas to the College towards the buildings in 1720.

Nathaniel Lord Crewe, Bishop of Durham, unasked, sent the College £100 towards the erection of their chapel.

On September 10, 1720, Samuel Cooke, M.A., Rector of Little Wittenham, Prebendary of Gloucester, and afterwards Archdeacon of Oxford, gave the College five guineas towards their buildings; and in November, 1714, he gave the College a study of books, consisting of 400 volumes.

Mr. Daniel Godwyne, of the City of London, who died in 1761, bequeathed by will to the College his books and papers, and several mathematical instruments.

Robert Burd Gabriel, a Fellow upon Dr. Clarke's foundation, gave a handsome grate for the use of the hall in 1784.

In a letter dated 1832, Walter Williams, " calling to remembrance that in a season of the greatest affliction under the blessing of Almighty God the means provided by the College greatly contributed to his support in life," bequeathed to the Provost and Fellows the sum of £500 to be disposed of as they should deem most conducive to the interests of the Society. The gift, which was subject to a life estate, and did not fall in till 1843, was expended in the purchase of the tithes of Hillmarton, in the county of Wilts.

On November 30, 1870, Dr. R. L. Cotton, the Provost of the College, presented the iron railings which at present stand at the entrance of the College.

The Rev. G. C. Bell, late Fellow and tutor, gave £50, and R. T. Tidswell, Esq., gave £100 for the payment of exhibitioners.

The Rev. James Hannay, late Fellow and Bursar, bequeathed £500 to the Fellows of the College to be employed at their discretion.

CHAPTER XI

CHAPEL — LIBRARY — HALL — THE GARDENS — PLATE — PICTURES — THE COLLEGE ARMS — REGISTERS — BIBLE-CLERKS — FELLOW-COMMONERS — THE RIVER — THE UNDERGRADUATE

The Chapel

The present chapel, like its two predecessors, was many years in building. Begun in 1720 with money left by Mrs. Margaret Alcorne, it was at least sixty-six years before it was completed with the plain internal fittings which it retained till 1864. The building was lit by windows only on the east and south; the walls were covered with a coating of stone-coloured paint begrimed with dust and gas; lofty box-like pews, too often the convenient shelter of irreverence, lined either side, and twice in each term, when the Provost preached a sermon, a somewhat loftier box was dragged into the middle of the chapel to serve as pulpit.

Dissatisfaction with this sordid state of things first took the shape of a scheme for the erection of a new chapel on the open side of the quadrangle, but fortunately this was set aside, and the plans of Mr. Burges for the renovation and decoration of the interior of the existing chapel were finally adopted. From first to last over £7,000 was expended on this work, of which more than £6,000 was contributed by members of the College. Begun in 1863, the chapel was reopened in 1864 with a sermon by Bishop Wilberforce, one of the Visitors of the College, but details continued to be carried out through several succeeding years. The final result is a glowing richness of decoration, and an elaborate scheme of iconography, to which it might be difficult to name a parallel. Mr. Burges retained unaltered the original shell, the proportions of which he pronounced to be of the highest merit, but he opened three windows on the north side corresponding to those on the south. The stucco ceiling was still further enriched by the addition of geometrical mouldings, and was divided into two compartments, with a dome in the centre. In the eastern compartment is represented the Fall of Man and the three theological virtues, Faith, Hope and Charity, together with the fourth virtue of Humility, which was required to complete the scheme. The western compartment represents the expulsion from the garden of Eden, and the subject is surrounded with representations of the four cardinal virtues—Justice, Temperance, Chastity and Fortitude.

At the angles of the dome are four kings, ancestors of our Lord—David, Solomon, Hezekiah, and Josiah.

The windows on the north side represent the Annunciation, the teaching in the Temple, and the women at the sepulchre; on the south side the Baptism, the offering of the wise men, and the Ascension. The eastern window is devoted to the Crucifixion, and the

THE CHAPEL

whole series of windows represents "Christ the Light of the World." Millais furnished a design for one of these, but the series was eventually designed by Mr. Henry Holiday, and carried out by Lavers and Barraud.

In the lunette over each window is a half-length figure of the prophet, whose words have been interpreted to refer to the event represented in the glass below. The four niches at the angles contain gilt statues of the four Evangelists, with a little painting above in grisaille, representing an event of their lives. Thus St. Matthew is called by our Lord from the money-changer's table, St. John looks into the sepulchre, St. Mark journeys by sea, and St. Luke paints the Virgin. In the arabesques at the sides the same idea is carried out by the introduction of their respective symbols, a money-changer's table, a chalice and serpent, an ink bottle and pen, and a pallet and brushes. The arabesques at the sides of the windows, executed by Mr. Smallfield, contain subjects from the *Benedicite*, and illustrate the various works of creation, the sentences referring to them being painted on the frieze above. Here are represented birds, beasts, and fishes, precious stones, the fruits of the earth, and man himself—all "the works of the Lord" are represented joining in the universal *Benedicite*. On the other hand, the words of the *Te Deum* inlaid in the panelling which runs round the chapel give the key to the procession of figures on a gold ground (the work of Mr. Holiday) which fill the space between panelling and windows; on the north side the heavenly host; on the south the types of human society, the company of the

Apostles, the fellowship of the Prophets, the army of martyrs, from the Innocents to Jerome of Prague, Latimer, and Hooper, and, finally, the Church throughout the world, whose various energy is symbolized by Augustine and Ambrose, the Empress Helena and Monica, Charlemagne and Benedict, Catherine of Sienna and Elizabeth of Hungary, Thomas Aquinas and Wycliffe, Luther and Pascal. The floor, in *opus vermiculatum*, completed some years later, is the counterpart of the ceiling. That represents the Degradation of Man, this his restitution in the Church; in the sacrarium the Harvest of the Sower; above the lectern the Western Church represented by its four doctors, and below it kings, writers, martyrs, builders, and saints, representatives of the Church in England. Above the altar is a predella painting of the entombment, and on one side of it a picture of St. Benet, the patron of the Benedictine Order; on the other of Sir Thomas Cookes, presenting as an offertory a model of his College. The latter is copied from a miniature in the possession of the Cookes family, and is said to be the best portrait of Sir Thomas in the possession of the College. The stalls are of walnut-wood inlaid with box, and the standards contain shields with the instruments of the Passion, while the animals carved upon the finials carry out the conception of the *Benedicite*. Professor Westwood expressed an opinion that there was no English building extant in which so much study has been devoted to a scheme of ornamental decoration, and such care given to the execution of details.

The windows were the gifts respectively of Miss

Bullock, Dr. Collis, Jesse Watts Russell, Esq., W. R. Holden, Esq., Rev. G. C. Fenwicke, and the tenants of the College.

Other noticeable objects in the chapel are (1) Two alabaster candelabra, given by Dr. Collis; (2) six bronze candelabra presented in memory of Warren Livingstone, U.S.A., a former Fellow-Commoner; these are now, with a praiseworthy simplicity and taste, adapted to the electric light, which is employed in the chapel as well as in all other parts of the Colleges; (3) the alabaster lectern, filleted by a group of youths, chanting the *Te Deum*, the gift of the scholars; (4) the lectern Bible in two volumes, the silver binding of which was designed by Mr. Burges, the gift of the present Bursar. The changes of 1864 included the addition of an organ, of considerable merit for its size; the organ scholar is an undergraduate member of the College, and the services on Sunday are rendered chorally.

The Library

The Library, which is a long and handsome gallery, extending the whole length of the front above the cloister, is adorned by some fine casts from the antique presented by Mr. Philip Pusey. For a college library it is of considerable size. It possesses but few MSS. or incunabula. By far the most important of these is the "History of the Black Prince," a poem in Norman-French by Chandos Herald, the final lines of which form the inscription on the monument of the Black Prince in Canterbury Cathedral. Of the valuable Clarke papers mention has already been made. Another 8vo. MS. is Dean Aldrich's treatise on "The Elements of Architecture." There are numerous architectural designs of Hawkesmoor and others for the reconstruction of Brasenose, Magdalen, and other colleges, as well as a large collection of works on architecture and classical antiquities. The most important is the series of designs for Whitehall Palace, executed by Inigo Jones or his pupil. There is also a copy of Palladio's work on "Architecture" (1601) which was his companion in Italy, of which the margins are filled with annotations in his hand, as is the case with several other books. These form part of the collection of Dr. Clarke, himself, like his friend Dr. Aldrich, an enthusiastic amateur architect. From the same source came the valuable collection of old English plays, and the still more valuable collection of pamphlets of the period of the Civil War, volumes of Laud pamphlets, volumes of Prynne pamphlets, the contemporaneous collection of Dr. Clarke's father, followed by many volumes of a later date, collected by himself. Indeed, the Library may be described as Dr. Clarke's, supplemented by Dr. Gower and other later donors—notably the present librarian—as well as by purchases of modern works made from the funds of the Library itself. Of Gloucester Hall books but few are traceable, and those of little interest to a modern taste, *e.g.*, Gesner's "Bibliotheca Universalis," Tig. 1545; the logical works of Zabarella (1608) and the like. The bibliophile of the present day will find greater interest in the unique copy of Goddard's "Neast of Waspes" (1615), or Alexander Hales on the "De Anima," Oxford, 1481, the gift of Clement Barksdale to Gloucester Hall; while ladies find a special charm in Carleton's "Thankful Remembrancer of God's Mercy," 1627, elaborately bound in velvet, covered with gold lace and seed pearls. In 1873 the College resolved to appropriate a portion of the funds of the Library to the special subject of Classical Archæology, and to create an Undergraduates' Library, both of which designs have been carried into effect.

The Hall

Sconcing exists at present at Worcester College exactly as it existed at Lincoln College in the years 1876 to 1879, according to the account given by the Rev. Andrew Clark in his "History of Lincoln College" in this series. In recent years there have been some signs of the decline of the custom. One of the rules existing at Worcester is to the effect that a man who is sconced and successfully floors the sconce—that is to say, drains it at one draught—may sconce the whole table. A sconce may be inflicted for obtaining a first-class in the schools, or for any other notable distinction. Grace is said by the junior scholar in Hall as soon as the seniority have reached the high table.

The grace before meat is the old Latin grace and somewhat long, and a custom, not commendable, has of late years grown up for the undergraduates to come in after its conclusion. The grace after meat, in which the founder was duly commemorated, has fallen into desuetude, the junior members, inclusive of the scholars, being permitted to quit the Hall, each at the conclusion of his own dinner, without waiting for the High Table or asking leave, as in other colleges. At present men sit in Hall in order of seniority, the scholars occupying a separate table. Dr. Bloxam, who was a member of the College *circa* 1826, tells us how in his days the tables were allotted according to the habits of their occupants. The table on the right was occupied by the gay men of the College, and was called the Sinners' Table. The table on the left was called the Smilers' Table. These formed a distinct set between the Sinners and the Saints, who occupied the table nearest the High Table on the left. The "Invitation Table," as it was more decorously and appropriately designated, survived into the seventies. The Bachelors, who then resided for their M.A. degree, used to appear in Hall in full evening dress, silk stockings, etc. Undergraduates, however, had left off dining in white neckcloths. The College Tonsor, an official whose salary was provided for in the original Statutes, and who was still in existence in 1860, was put in requisition to do the necessary hairdressing.

The Hall, till 1877 a plain though admirably proportioned room, was in that year decorated in accordance with the designs of the late Mr. Burges, at a cost of some £2,000, of which about £1,100 was subscribed by members of the College. Dr. Gabriel's grate was replaced by a handsome marble fireplace; the walls were lined with richly panelled woodwork, inlaid with the armorial bearings of members of the College, past and present; a handsome buffet was given by Mr. Greswell; and a window representing banqueting scenes from Homer, Virgil, Shakespeare, and Milton was contributed by the junior members of the College.

The College Gardens

The College is surrounded on all sides, except that facing the street, with a belt of gardens. The garden to which the public have access is one of the chief

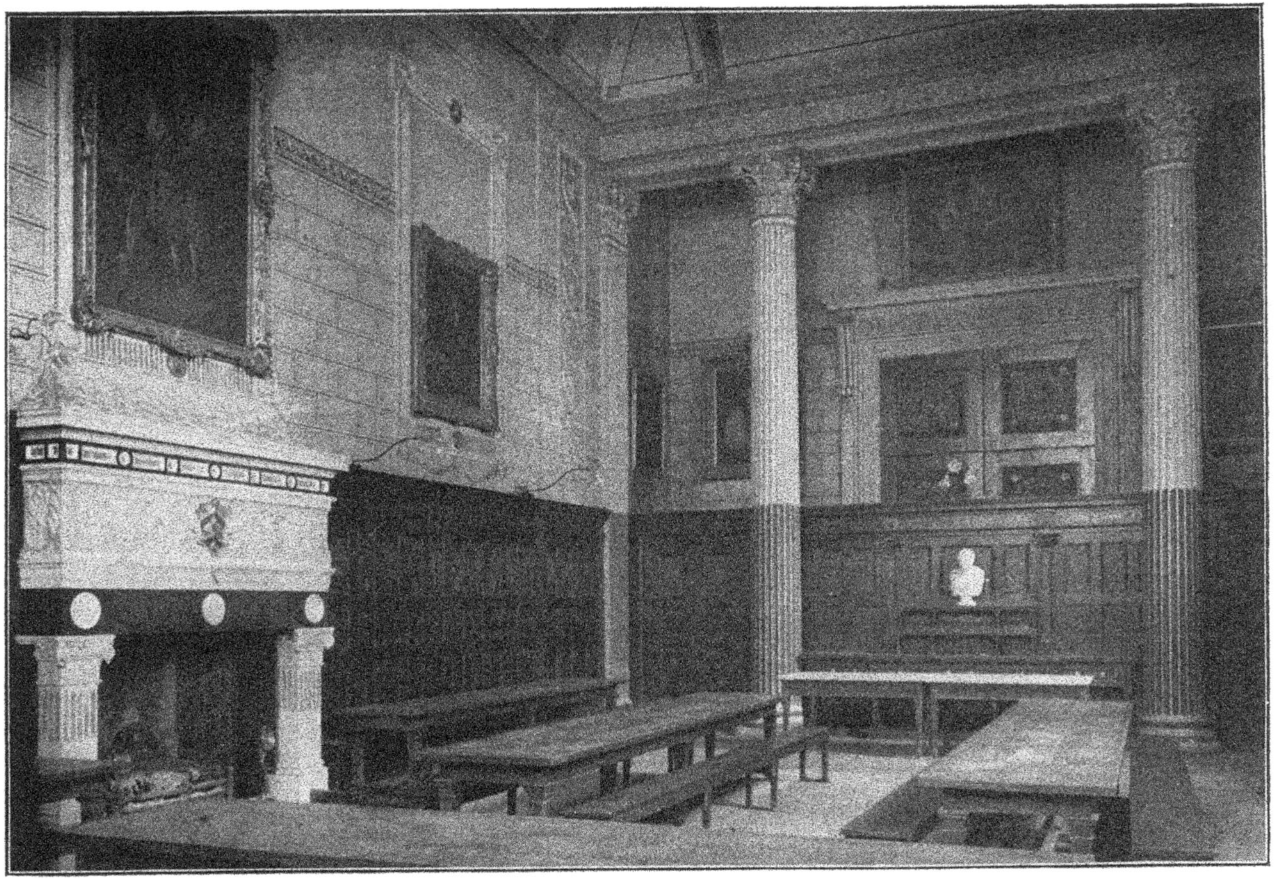

Ex[illegible] Camera Club

beauties of the College. The site was purchased of Mr. Thomas Wrench in 1741 for the sum of £850. In former days it was nothing but a water-meadow, intersected with lanes of water from the adjacent river. In the earlier part of this century a snipe or a stray Witham pheasant might be flushed in its solitudes. It was laid out in its present form by Richard Greswell during his Bursarship in 1827. In the spring, when the flowering shrubs and trees are in bloom, the beauty of the gardens is at its height, but at all seasons the tree-shaded landscape, bounded by the Pool, possesses what is for Oxford a unique charm.

Worcester is almost the only College in Oxford which possesses a fives court. It used to boast of two. One —an open court—was situated in the Fellows' Garden, for the use of the older members; the other is in the principal garden—a covered building with a gallery of the usual type. It was built about the middle of the present century as a present of the Common Room to the junior members of the Society, whose other recreations have changed with the fashion of the day— archery, bowls, croquet, lawn-tennis. The Pool, in which are some fair jack, tench, etc., has for many years been tenanted by a pair of swans. Peacocks were kept till insomnia and ruined flower-beds rendered them unendurable. A fine eagle, brought by Mr. Muckleston from Norway, was at one time kept in the Fellows' Garden, and still in its glass case recalls the memory of a small clique of Scandinavian enthusiasts in days before Norway had become the fashion.

Plate

Among the plate in the possession of the College several pieces have a special value as relics of Gloucester Hall. One of these is a silver tankard, the gift of Philip Harcourt in 1696; it weighs 22 ozs. 16 dwts. Another was the gift of Viscount Scudamore in 1697. Other pieces of Gloucester Hall plate referred to in the Benefactors' Book were the gift of Robert Lowndes in 1695, and of William Pym in 1704. There are in all thirteen large tankards or sconce-pots which contain on an average three pints. These are known to undergraduate members by various names, such as Old Tom, and Old Tom's Brother, both given by John Cookes; Bell Top, given by Biddulph; and Flat Top, the gift of the said Philip Harcourt in 1716. These are all in point of size eclipsed by "Blue Peter," a tankard given in 1866 by ten undergraduates—Messrs. Scholefield, Bath, Sumerfield, Page, Scurfield, Penfold, Wood, Rowland, Hartley, and Lawrence. It weighs 83 ounces, and holds seven pints. There are also fifty-four silver pint pots, and eight half-pints. The finest piece in the possession of the College is a grace-cup, the legacy of Dr. George Clarke, who was "almost our founder," as the grateful inscription it bears testifies. It is a very fine two-handled silver-gilt cup weighing 113 ozs. 7 dwts.

Some pieces of the Common Room plate, with their donors, deserve enumeration. A large silver-gilt punch-bowl, the gift of Sir H. O. Keate in 1720. A "soup-dish," presented by Charles Wake Jones in 1744; two gilded goblets, by J. Collins in 1775; a silver beaker, by Edward Amphlett in 1816; a large tureen, 1817; an urn, 1819; a claret-jug, by Mr. Bullock in 1858; a coin cup, by Mr. Burges in 1864; a Hannap cup, by Mr. Hole in 1875; a large salver in memory of Mr. Blaney Wright, late Fellow, with other donations by living members of the College.

In 1878 the Common Room was broken into, and the burglar, after refreshing himself from the College cellar, carried off a hamperful of plate, carefully wrapped in a moiety of the door curtain. The burglar was subsequently captured, and the plate recovered on his indication of the locality—Slough Railway-station—where he had deposited it. Some of the plate still bears the marks of the rough handling it had received, and the moiety of the curtain is still left hanging in the Common Room as a memento.

The Sacramental Plate is not remarkable either for character or date. It consists of a flagon, two chalices, two patens (all without inscriptions), two large patens "in memory of the Hon. H. R. Skeffington" (1846), and a silver-gilt alms-dish, given in 1855 in memory of Antony Gibbs.

PICTURES

The more valuable and interesting of the pictures and portraits belonging to the College hang in the Provost's lodgings. In the dining-room of that house are portraits of Dr. Byrom Eaton, Principal of Gloucester Hall 1662 to 1692; of Dr. Woodroffe, Principal from 1692 to 1711; of Dr. Richard Blechynden, his successor, and then Provost of Worcester College from 1714 to 1736; of Dr. William Gower (by T. Gibson),

Provost 1736 to 1777; and of Dr. R. L. Cotton, Provost 1839 to 1880. There is also a portrait of Dr. George Clarke, by Sir Godfrey Kneller. But the portrait of greatest interest is that of the learned antiquary, William Camden, the patron of Degory Wheare, and founder of the Chair of Ancient History, of which the latter was first occupant. This was doubtless the picture which William Camden presented to Degory Wheare, and which Degory Wheare acknowledged in the following letter dated March 12, 1622:

"Verisimilem tui similitudinem artificiosa graphide depictam (multo adfectu cultuque multo tabulam exosculatus) nudius tertius accepi et hac ipsa hora prolixæ etiam tuæ largitatis portionem haud minutam decem puto libras meis necessitatibus supplendis inopiæque sublevandæ commodissimum a te missas. Vide igitur quantifariam te tuaque bonitate jam fruor. . . . In cubiculo tabula isthaec novella corporis orisque tui venustam repræsentans figuram venerabundos sæpiuscule detinet oculos."*

Pictures of far greater value, though not of the same intrinsic interest to the College, were bequeathed by Treadway Russell Nash, formerly Fellow, and author of the "History of Worcestershire." They include, besides a celebrated landscape by Ruysdaal, two pictures by John von Hensen, a "Nativity" by Bassano, a "Last Supper" which is attributed to Ricci, and another picture by Moucheron.

In the Hall.—Besides a fish picture of the Dutch school, the Hall contains twelve portraits, among them those of Sir Thomas Cookes, Dr. Clarke, Lady Holford,

* "Camdeni Epistolæ," London, 1691, p. 337.

Provost Sheffield, Mrs. Eaton, Dean Landon, Dr. Cotton (by Boxall), Bishop Binney of Nova Scotia, Bishop Harding of Bombay, and Professor Thorold Rogers.

In the Library lobby is a portrait of Sir Thomas Cookes, given by Samuel Wanley, formerly Fellow. In 1773, by special resolution, recorded in the College register, this picture was sent to R. E. Pine, of Bath, to copy. An artist who visited Worcester College in 1785, and whose manuscript notes of his tour are in the Bodleian, relates a curious story as to this portrait. He says that it was sent to Bath to be copied by Mr. Pine, who returned a "picture totally unlike, the original being tall and thin, this rather short and fat. . . ." He adds a description of the picture "in a purple dress, hair like a wig, sword and hat in his left hand, standing surprised at the bust of Alfred—a most shocking performance." Whatever credit we may attach to the story, we are compelled to assent to the criticism. Samuel Wanley was elected Fellow in 1737, on an occasion when there were only two candidates capable of being elected, and one of them was excluded in consequence of a disorder in his understanding.

In the Senior Common Rooms there are several paintings and a few prints of former members of the College. The paintings include two pictures given by Treadway Russell Nash in 1811: a portrait of Richard Greswell (presented by the Misses Greswell), and of James Hannay, who were both—the latter for many years—Bursars of the College; a portrait on panel, dated 1666, the subject doubtful; and portraits of two Common Room men, one of whom—Preston—was the

College servant of Thomas de Quincey, and continued in the service of the Common Room till 1865. There are engravings of Richard Lovelace, Thomas Coryate, Samuel Foote, and Dr. Miller—a former Bampton lecturer—and a portrait of de Quincey which has a peculiar interest, as it was given to the present Bursar by his daughter, and by him presented to the Common Room. There are also two pencil sketches of H. O. Coxe, late Bodley's librarian, by the late Rev. R. A. J. Tyrwhitt.

The Arms of the College

The arms of the College are stated in Gutch's Wood to be: Argent, two chevrons gules between six martlets gules, and the arms of Ulster. Crest: a hand, armed, grasping a sword. These are the arms of Cookes of Bentley, and are apparently the proper arms of the College, but Oxford stationers persist in tricking our arms in a different way, namely: Or, two chevrons gules between six martlets sable; badge, argent, a hand paleways gules. There can be no doubt that these arms are erroneous. They more closely resemble the arms of Cookes of Norgrove: Argent, two chevrons, gules, between six martlets, sable. The arms of Cookes of Bentley are not those which originally belonged to that family, but are derived from the family of Jennet. The original arms of the Cookes family were: Barry, of six argent and sable, in chief three mullets, gules. It appears to be a nice heraldic point how far the College is entitled to bear the bloody hand of Ulster of the Founder's Coat. The badge of Ulster is often omitted, as, for instance, in the University Calendar.

THE COLLEGE BOOKS

The following are the registers and books which have been or are at present kept by the College. Scanty as they are, they constitute the principal materials for the history of the College since 1714.

(a) A book which bears the name of the "Worcester College Register." It is a very large folio volume, bound in vellum. It was commenced in the Provostship of Richard Blechynden. The first entry in this book is dated February 26, 172¾, and has reference to the purchase of Whitfield. About the middle of the eighteenth century, as Dr. Gower was becoming an old man, the entries become very incomplete and infrequent; often two or three years pass without a single note. When Dr. Sheffield became Provost in 1777 he discontinued the record entirely, and there is a lacuna in the official records of the College from this date up to 1796. There are hardly any notes in any of the College books written by Dr. Sheffield, and such as there are are mostly confined to criticisms of his predecessors' entries. The book was taken up again by Dr. Landon, and towards the middle of the nineteenth century the character of the entries becomes once more full and complete. Originally certain miscellaneous matters, such as advances to the Bursar from the College chest, were entered in the book; but at the present day it is exclusively a record of the minutes of the proceedings of "General College Meetings." Until the year 1866 there was held only one stated General Meeting in the year, on St. Andrew's Day. Since that time a second meeting has been held, in June.

(b) A second volume may be referred to as the "Benefactors' Book." It is a large octavo, a little smaller in size than a half-sheet of foolscap, and is bound in leather. It is earlier in date than the Register, as it commences with the foundation of the College, in 1714. There is writing at both ends of the book, but the larger proportion of the pages remain blank. No entries have been made for the past century—that is to say, since 1778.

At one end the volume begins with a list of benefactions: "In grateful remembrance of such as do good to Worcester College their names and benefactions are here registered." The last entry in this part is in 1753. The greater part of it has been copied almost verbatim in Gutch's edition of Wood's "Colleges of Oxford."

A few pages further on Dr. Sheffield begins an attempt at keeping the record of his Provostship, but there is only one entry, under date December, 1777, embodying some resolutions as to the mode of keeping the College accounts. The other end of the volume opens with an account of the plate "which was given to the Hall before it was a College, and remains there now." On the second page is an account of plate given to Worcester College since its foundation. The last entry is dated 1720. (See Plate.) A few pages further on is an account in draft and fair copy of money given by the College in charity 1776 to 1778. (See Bible Clerks.)

(c) The third volume is exactly similar in appearance to the Benefactors' Book. At one end it contains a list of College officers and Fellows and scholars from 1714 to 1774. At this point, and in some cases at an earlier date, the entries are divided, and the scholars and Fellows are entered separately under their several foundations. The latest entry is under date 1778, a year after Dr. Sheffield was appointed Provost. There are also a few miscellaneous entries, copies of decrees in Chancery and of the instruments appointing various Provosts, together with an opinion on the case of Samuel Foote. The last entry of the kind is an account of the dispute which led to an appeal to the Visitor on the question of the Cookes Fellows and scholars in 1775. At the other end is an incomplete list of commoners admitted to the College from 1714. With his usual consistency, Dr. Sheffield gave up keeping the list in 1777, and since then the list of commoners has been kept in a separate volume.

(d) This is a large quarto volume, which contains a list of matriculations at the College. The earlier entries are incomplete, and they are not contemporary. They were compiled at the beginning of the Provostship of Dr. Cotton.

(e) The Buttery Books are believed to contain the only complete list of members of the College. These Buttery Books are a complete series from the foundation of the College in 1714. The books have an official character, because the name of every new member of the College as he enters is officially entered by the Provost. It may be observed, as an interesting illustration of the conservatism of Oxford usage in small details, that the title "Dominus," indicated by the abbreviation "Ds.," though a mysterious and unintelligible symbol to the buttery clerk, is still faithfully retained by him before the name of every Bachelor of Arts—a use now almost obsolete, it is believed, at Oxford, but still retained in the Cambridge Class Lists.

Bible Clerks

In 1821 two Bible clerks were established at the College. Their duties were first to deliver out from the Dean the subject of College exercises, and to collect the exercises and deliver them to the Dean, with the names of defaulters; to say grace in the College hall before and after dinner; to look out and mark the lessons for the day in chapel; and to write out the forms of College testimonials. For performing these services they were to receive the following remuneration: £1 on the entry of a gentleman commoner, 9s. on the entry of a commoner, 2s. 6d. for every grace that was granted, and 5s. for College testimonials. This was not the first occasion of a tax levied for eleemosynary purposes. In the eighteenth century there had been a charity fund in the College, to which every member was expected or compelled to subscribe. The money was paid out to various charities, such as the University Boys' and Girls' Charity Schools, and the accounts for the years 1777 to 1781 are contained in the benefactors' book.

These payments had been allowed to lapse, and they were now revived for the maintenance of the Bible clerks. Two rooms were fitted up for the Bible clerks on No. 1 staircase rent free. The Bible clerkships were abolished in 1867. Their duties were divided, and the task of writing College testimonials and receipt of the fee for the same devolved upon the College messenger. The most distinguished of the Bible clerks was Mr. Richard Robinson, who subsequently was elected to a scholarship, and afterwards became Fellow of Queen's. He was a great authority on the history of Oxford in the eighteenth century. By a singular coincidence the Bible clerk who was contemporary with Robinson was Cruso, and anyone who climbed No. 1 staircase would find the names of Robinson Cruso inscribed over the doors at the top.

Fellow-Commoners

Worcester College is now almost, if not quite, the only College in Oxford which preserves the academic grade of fellow-commoners. At one time they were young men of fortune, who desired an exemption from the stricter discipline of undergraduate life. At the present day they are generally men of maturer years than the average undergraduate, whose tastes and age render them better fitted to consort with the seniority. In the early days of the College they were generally as numerous and sometimes more numerous than the commoners. At the present day there are not often more than four or five members of this status. They wear a peculiar gown, and are a survival of the " Commensales superioris ordinis " of Gloucester Hall days. It would be interesting to know when they adopted their present title. Throughout the eighteenth century they always bore the title of " gentleman-commoner," the title they bore in most other Colleges to which they were admitted. At present and, at any rate, for the past fifty years they have been known as " fellow-commoners," and as such are registered in the buttery books.

The River

Though the small numbers of the College have always prevented it from taking the first place on the river, yet, considering this fact, its achievements in this direction have almost always been creditable, and at times distinguished and even brilliant. The appearance of a Worcester College crew on the river is almost synchronous with the commencement of College boating. In the first College race of 1824, of which the history has come down to us, a Worcester College man joined with a Thames waterman to give gallant assistance to Brasenose College when that College beat Jesus, the only other College to have a boat on the river. In the following year there was a race between Exeter, Christchurch, Worcester, and Balliol, in which Worcester ended third; and these Colleges, with Brasenose and Jesus, may be considered as the pioneers of the modern eights. Thomas Garnier, a member of the College, rowed in the first contest between the Universities in 1829. He was son of an old Worcester man—Thomas Garnier, who was Dean of Winchester, and lived to the patriarchal age of ninety-seven. Thomas Garnier the second was no less distinguished in the Church than on the river, and he lived to occupy the Deaneries of Ripon and Lincoln.

The history of rowing at Oxford is exceptionally obscure for the next few years, and we obtain the next record of the doings of the Worcester crew with the commencement of the Worcester College Boat Club minute-book in 1844. There must be very few clubs in Oxford which possess a minute-book which goes back

THE RIVER

for more than half a century, and the Worcester book is only seven years younger than the celebrated records of the Brasenose Boat Club.

The history of rowing at the College since that date has been one of remarkable vicissitudes. Briefly, it may be said that the College boating records are relieved by five good periods.

1. The first lasted from 1845 to 1853. In the first of these years we made four bumps and ended tenth. In 1846 we again made four bumps, and ended sixth. In 1847 we were fourth, and in 1848 we were second, both in the eights and the torpids. This is the highest position we ever attained on the river. We maintained this high place for several years. In 1850 we put two eights on which ended fourth and eighteenth. In 1851 we were fourth, and in 1852 and in 1853 we were third. For the next thirteen years the College took very little part in University rowing. We went down three places in the year of the Crimean war, and then took our boat off, a very common practice in those days. In the next few years we were often without either a torpid or an eight on the river.

2. The three years' captaincy of Mr. Banks (several years Treasurer of the University Boat Club) formed our second period of prosperity. It began with the torpids of 1866, when three bumps were made, giving occasion for the first bump supper of which there is a record in the minute-book. In the next two years we went up nine places in the eights, an achievement which we have recently rivalled. The end of 1866 saw us eighth in the torpid and tenth in the eights. We sent an eight and a four to the Paris regatta this year. In

1868 we ended eighth in the torpid and sixth in the eights. Then followed a five years' period of depression, in which we were never very low and never very high.

3. 1873 was memorable as the year in which sliding-seats were first used in the University Boat Race. They were not generally used in the eights that followed, but on the third night of the eights Worcester went into a boat with sliding seats. The result was startling. Immediately ahead Merton had caught Exeter, but Worcester pulled on and bumped Magdalen, thus going up three places in one night. In the following year the eights were rowed in two divisions, and Worcester went up to tenth.

4. In 1879 and 1880 Worcester had another series of remarkable successes with her torpid, going up no less than twelve places in the two years. In 1880 they made seven bumps. This was the first time any crew had made that number of bumps in the history of the torpids; their success in this respect was followed by Lincoln, which made seven bumps in 1881. At the end of 1880 we were eighth on the river in the torpids, and twelfth in the eights.

5. The fifth period of rowing prosperity in the College began in 1898. In the eights of 1898 and 1899 we have made ten bumps, and ten in the torpids of 1899 and 1900, a total of twenty bumps in a period of two years.

It may also be mentioned that the College secured the Clinker Cup in 1890, 1892, and 1894.

The books contain a considerable amount of additional information which throws a very interesting light on Oxford rowing. In early years the leader of the boat was always Stroke. A captain was at that date unknown, and the Stroke was an elected officer, supposed to be the best all-round oar in the boat. The first captain of the club was elected in 1845 at a comparatively early date. Some colleges retained the elected Stroke to a much later date, and in the Queen's boat Stroke was the titular head of the boat as late as 1862. In 1845 Oriel College lent us their Torpid, and the kindness was gracefully recognised by the presentation of a College flag to the Oriel boat by the Worcester coxswain. In 1848 there was a formal ceremony of christening on the launching of a new boat named the *Queen of the May*. The stroke made two attempts to break a bottle of port over the bows of the boat, but only succeeded in cutting his hand. In the University fours of 1850 the Worcester boat beat Balliol, which was stroked by the Mr. Justice Chitty of later days. A better race "had not occurred on the river within the memory of the oldest inhabitant." The difference between ancient and modern rowing is emphasized by an entry under date 1852, where it is mentioned that Mr. Colpoys, "though he had only been accustomed to pull in the sea, most gallantly did acquit himself on the river." In 1855 the boat which had been used for the inter-University race was raffled for among the Colleges, and was won by the Worcester Boat Club, which took three shares out of forty. In 1862 the club was in great financial difficulties. An alliance was made with the cricket club, which foreshadowed the later system of amalgamated clubs. It was proposed to send all who refused to join the club " to Coventry," but the resolution was happily negatived. In Lent, 1881, our boat was involved in the destruction of the newly-completed University boat-house by fire.

The College Colours

The College colours have undergone frequent modifications. In 1846 they were a white jersey with pink stripes, and straw hat with pink-and-white ribbons. In 1851 a pink cross was added to the jersey. In 1855 there was a complete change to puce velvet caps and puce-trimmed jerseys. In 1863 pink and white entwined were the colours of the club, and in 1866 the eight returned to a pink-and-white jersey. In 1866 a black blazer trimmed with pink cord was substituted for the white blazer. The torpid was to wear one pink cross and the eight two pink crosses on the jersey. The straw hat was black and white trimmed with broad pink. This was eventually changed, in 1875, to the present black and pink. A black-and-pink jersey was also introduced, and the present uniform dates (with but slight alterations) from 1887.

University Oars

The following have at various times represented the University: T. Garnier 1829, E. G. C. Griffiths 1847, E. Sykes 1848-50, W. Nixon 1851, A. Hooke 1854-55, J. H. Fish and E. S. Carter 1867-68, E. C. Malan 1871-72, and W. D. Craven 1876. Besides these, J. Cohen, J. S. Gibbons, J. M. Mulgan, and A. S. Orlebar rowed in the trial eights, and H. S. Chesshire won the University sculls two years in succession.

College Prizes

There have been an exceptional number of College prizes for rowing in the College at various times.

Cups were given for a four-oar race in 1845, and before this date oars and rudders had been given for the same race. In 1865 challenge cups were substituted for prizes in this race. Two of them were presented by Jocelyn Barnes and R. G. Scurfield, and two more were purchased by subscription. They are still competed for annually.

In 1852 Henry Kingsley, the novelist, presented a pair of silver oars for the winners of the College pair-oars. Of these, only the bow-oar survives. In the same year Mr. Baumgarten presented a pair of sculls for College skiff races, and subsequently he presented a second pair. These seem to have disappeared at an early date, and in 1859 Mr. Daniel presented another pair, which were competed for regularly for many years. But early in the seventies they disappeared. In 1879 a London pawnbroker communicated with the secretary of the club to the effect that the sculls were in his possession, and they were redeemed by the kindness of a Fellow of the College. Both pairs have now disappeared. In 1860 the Rev. E. C. Adams presented the club with a pair of silver Junior Pair-oars, which are still rowed for. Four silver oars and a rudder were presented in 1874 for torpid fours, but one oar has been lost. To complete the catalogue of College prizes, a single fives challenge-cup was presented in 1870, and two double challenge fives cups were presented in 1864 by J. C. Scholefield. A challenge-cup for a quarter of a mile was presented in 1891 by W. E. Gibbons, and a challenge-cup was presented in 1863 for a two miles' steeplechase across country. It is now given for a two miles' race on the flat.

The Barge

The College first hired a barge in March, 1847, at the rent of £8 per annum. It retained this barge till December, 1855, when it was resolved to give it up as a useless expense. This was a time when the College had no boat on the river, and was very heavily in debt. From 1855 to 1871 we were apparently without a barge on the river, but in 1871 it was decided to hire a barge from Mrs. Beasley for £28 per annum. The barge was situated at the entrance to the Cherwell. It was fitted out at considerable expense, but it does not appear to have given satisfaction. In 1878 it was resolved to abandon Mrs. Beasley's barge, and take one from Salter. At the same time an effort was made to secure a new position for our barge in the place it at present occupies. Talboys at that date occupied the site, and refused to move. The help of the Thames Conservancy had to be invoked, and Talboys received notice to abandon the spot within thirty-six hours. Talboys, being deserted by the Sheriff and Town Clerk of Oxford, whose assistance he had invoked, did so, and our new barge was put into position at the end of the summer term of 1879. It was a barge which had once belonged to New College. In 1882 it was presented with a flag by the kindness of the Provost's family, a gift which has several times been renewed.

The old barge caused a considerable amount of

trouble. Mrs. Beasley thought she had been hardly treated, and at one time litigation was threatened. Eventually it was sold to John Bossom, and departed to the upper river. An agreement, however, was made that the College should have the use of it in any year when they were compelled to practise on the upper river owing to the floods. The occupation of the new barge involved the construction of a path across the Cherwell, to which the various Colleges which owned barges on this side of the river contributed.

The present barge was purchased by subscription, and was delivered to the College on May 10, 1887.

The Undergraduate

It is especially difficult to generalize about the characteristics of the undergraduate population of a College, because there is no element which is so mutable. The writer is compelled almost of necessity to draw upon the experience of the three or four years when he was an undergraduate, and to generalize from that experience to a whole century or more. Nevertheless, we may with some diffidence lay down some of the more salient characteristics of the College which have persisted for the 186 years that the College has existed. The most striking, undoubtedly, is the great extent to which it has drawn from the sons of the clergy for its undergraduates, and recruited the clergy from its graduates. It is easier to state the fact than give the reason for it. But a clerical tradition, when once established, is very persistent. The clergy and the English county families are the only classes of English society which persistently and habitually send their sons to the University, and in this way father succeeds son at the same College. In the case of Worcester the tendency has been especially marked, because the Church is a natural vocation for the sons of the upper middle classes who have received a University training, and have no particular tradition or influence to lead them to launch out in other quarters. And in the second place the College itself has always been noted for the number of good Churchmen it has had among its Fellows and tutors. Thomas Harward, John Miller, Richard Greswell, Provost Cotton, and Dean Burgon (who, though not a Fellow, was closely identified with Worcester), were all well-known Churchmen, and had thoroughly won the confidence of the clergy. Thus, of M.A.'s on the books of the College in a single recent year taken at random, we find that the clergy are to the laity as three to one—150 clergy and 49 laymen.

The second characteristic of the College, which is common among the larger colleges, but not so common among the smaller colleges, unless they also have a local tradition, is the persistence of the family tradition. There are a very large number of families which have sent five, six, or seven of their members to the College. The instances in which father and son have come to the College are extremely numerous, and there are a considerable number of cases in which a family has been represented at the College even to the third generation. There has scarcely ever been a time at which the College has not had some of the founder's kin among its members, and that long after the pecuniary advantages of that status had been abolished. The opening

THE UNDERGRADUATE

of scholarships and the spread of University education, together with the general poverty of the clergy, have all tended in recent years to dissipate the family tradition, but at the present day we can still speak of it as an existing fact.

The local tradition has always been rather slight at the College. It is true that the connection with Bromsgrove, and so with Worcestershire, as enjoined by the will of Sir Thomas Cookes, has been preserved to the present day; and there have been generally at least two or three Bromsgrove scholars among the undergraduate members of the College. But Commoners have not followed the scholars, and at the present day Worcester has perhaps fewer local ties than any of the old-established colleges; and in the last few years even the supply of Bromsgrove scholars has failed.

Such abiding influences in the life of a college as these serve to give it a more permanent character than the majority of colleges enjoy. The chief characteristic of the life of the College may be described by the Aristotelian term αὐτάρκεια. To a marvellous extent it finds itself and its own society sufficient for itself. The remote position of the College has always had an influence on its history. In the seventeenth century, when the grace for his degree was asked for Matthew Griffith, his absence from St. Mary's was excused on the ground that "ob distantiam loci et contrarios ventos campanæ sonitum audire non potuit."

At a later date this remoteness earned for the College the name of "Botany Bay," and the first Proctor who was appointed from Worcester was often met with derisive inquiries as to the situation of his College.

That name has fortunately disappeared, unfortunately to be replaced in recent years by one less euphonious and less reasonable. But the facts which gave it the name are still in existence. The Worcester undergraduate hardly participates at all in anything except the athletic life of Oxford. It has had only three officers in the Union Society in the ninety years the Union has existed, a President, a Librarian, and a Secretary. Its absence in the political, literary, and social clubs of the University is quite as conspicuous, and it takes almost as little part in the struggle for the intellectual honours of the University, though its position in the class lists is nearly always respectable and often honourable.

It certainly compensates for these disadvantages—if disadvantages they are to be called—in a strong sense of corporate unity. A small college that is self-centred is necessarily social, and Worcester has probably surpassed all other colleges in the number and variety of its social institutions. At times its clubs have seemed to be almost as numerous as its members. There have been wine clubs, breakfast clubs, literary clubs, debating clubs, socialist clubs, individualist clubs, church clubs, and æsthetic clubs, within the very short memory of the present writer. It has had clubs called after all the literary heroes the College has produced. It has had a club named after its founder; it has had clubs named after philosophers of antiquity; and, not satisfied with these, it has had recourse to the birds of the air and the beasts of the field and the days of the week to typify the infinite variety of its social life.

A mere catalogue would be wearisome, and might

exceed the limits of the volume. We will be satisfied with naming the most important. First in antiquity and in its corporate character comes the debating society. At present it forms part of the amalgamated clubs. Its early minute-books have disappeared, but it is at least fifty years old, and in its early days its proceedings were modelled on those of Parliament. It was reconstituted in the seventies, and has flourished continuously since that date. The second is the Lovelace Club, the only literary club in the College which can lay any claim to permanence. It meets weekly during term time on Sunday nights, and generally numbers a dozen or more members. At one time its membership was confined to those on the College foundation, but this restriction has been long since abolished. It has only one official, the Secretary, and no regular subscription. The ordinary course is for one member to read a paper, and the Secretary replies, and the other members take part in the discussion. There are only two occasions on which it has been completely at a loss. On the first a well-known member read a learned and ingenious paper on a certain Russian novelist. The members got up one after the other, and confessed that though much interested in the paper, they had till that evening never heard of the novelist, and had been unable to acquire information as to him or his works. It was not till some time afterwards that it transpired that the novelist and his novels only existed in the imagination of the reader, who had played an elaborate hoax upon the club. The second occasion was when a most distinguished stranger was announced to read a paper on William Wordsworth. However, there was some misunderstanding, and the stranger read on William Watson. He was considerably perplexed to understand why it was that member after member of the club got up and launched out into elaborate comparisons between William Watson and William Wordsworth.

An interesting offshoot of the Lovelace Club was the De Quincey Club, which was founded about 1892, though it existed at an earlier date under the name of the Anthology Club. It sought to include a wider circle than the Lovelace, and it was more popular and less literary. For some time there was a keen rivalry between the two clubs, but there was scarcely room for both, and as its original founders departed, the De Quincey gradually failed, till it totally disappeared in 1896. There are two other social clubs which deserve mention. The first is the "O. K." breakfast club. "O. K." is the telegraphic signal for "All right." This breakfasts weekly on Sunday morning. It consists of about eight members, and is confined almost entirely to the leading athletic men in the College. It is certainly one of the most ancient of the College clubs, and there are no breaks in its continuity. The second is the Kingsley Club, which was founded about the close of 1895. It celebrates a dinner two or three times a term in Hall, and this is followed by a wine; one of its features is that each of its members brings a guest from outside the College. It is to be hoped that this element will preserve it from decay; but even in the short period of its existence it has not always found it possible to keep up a sufficiency of members.

It may be said generally of the College that it delights to observe the mean. It is neither wholly devoted to athletics nor to the work of the schools. Its activities are very varied, and in almost every department of University life it maintains a very respectable position. The same may be said of the after-life of its members. It has been responsible for hardly any politicians. Of its three most distinguished public men two have been hanged, and the third only saved himself from a similar fate by meeting his death in a hand-to-hand fight. The wise Worcester man has since then avoided these perils:

" Non enim gazæ neque consularis
　　Summovet lictor miseros tumultus
　　Mentis et curas laqueata circum
　　　　Tecta volantis."

In the Church it has numbered many distinguished and able, but hardly any celebrated, clergy. At the Bar, the most popular profession after the Church, the greater part of its members have been content to remain among the juniors, and we think that not a single Worcester man has reached the English Bench. Likewise in literature, if one excepts a few distinguished men, its affections have gone out chiefly towards local antiquities and poetry. The College porter in his morning rounds, hammering on each staircase door with the traditional wooden mallet, continues the echo of the old Benedictine usage in the modern College; and something of the Benedictine spirit seems to linger round its ancient walls, and to imbue its members with a spirit of peacefulness and contentment, enabling them to recognise that it is not always the most ambitious or the most powerful who do the best service to the State.

The Cricket Field

The remoteness of the old cricket field at Cowley, and the difficulty of securing proper football grounds, has been in the past a considerable hindrance to College athletics. Under these circumstances a plan was formed, with the co-operation of the Provost and the College authorities, of converting the seven-acre meadow which lies to the south-west of the Pool into a cricket ground. The scheme had for many years been existent in a nebular state; but it was not till 1897 that the work was actually begun. As the meadow lay very low, and was beneath the level of the adjacent canal, it was necessary to drain it and raise its surface at a cost of about £1,100. A further sum of £865 has been spent on the erection of a pavilion in the south-east corner of the field. The pavilion has been built after a design by T. Tyrwhitt, Esq., Fellow-Commoner of the College. The sum is being raised by subscriptions from past and present members of the College, and up to the present time about £1,400 has been collected. The new cricket ground, though somewhat small, promises well, and is certainly one of the most picturesque in Oxford. A cricket match between past and present members of the College has been arranged for June 25, 1900, when the subscribers will have an opportunity of seeing the new field.

APPENDICES

A.—AUTHORITIES

THE following are the most important printed papers which have dealt with the history of Worcester College and its predecessors:

The History and Antiquities of the Colleges and Halls of Oxford, by Anthony Wood, with a continuation, by J. Gutch, 1786, pp. 629-639.

A History of the Colleges and Halls of Oxford, by A. Chalmers, F.S.A., 1810, pp. 428-437.

The Colleges of Oxford, edited by A. Clark (Worcester College, by the Rev. C. H. O. Daniel, pp. 425-448), 1892.

Ingram's Memorials of Oxford.

A Bygone Oxford, by Francis Goldie, S.J., pp. 27, 28.*

Burgon's Arms of the Colleges of Oxford.

Tanner's Notitia Monastica.*

Gloucester College, by the Rev. C. H. O. Daniel (Transactions of the Bristol and Gloucestershire Archæological Society, vol. xvi.).*

Proceedings of the Oxford Architectural and Historical Society, 1886, No. 32, pp. 48-57.

* These deal only with the Gloucester College period.

Dugdale's Monasticon Anglicanum (enlarged edition, 1823), vol. iv., pp. 403-409.*
Wood's City of Oxford—vol. ii., Colleges and Halls (O. H. S., ed. A. Clark).*

In addition to the above, Brian Twyne (Arch. Univ. Oxon) is a manuscript authority for the history of Gloucester College. Vols. xx.-xxiv. have been used in the first four chapters of the present volume. Wood's account is based almost entirely upon Twyne's manuscripts. The other manuscript authorities are referred to under the chapters in which they are used.

The following general authorities, amongst others, have been used in the course of the volume :

Maxwell Lyte's History of the University of Oxford.
Rashdall's Mediæval Universities.
Foster's Alumni Oxonienses.
Taunton's Black Monks.
Wood's Athenæ Oxonienses and Fasti Oxonienses.
The Dictionary of National Biography.
Reyner's De Apostolatu Benedictino.
Register of the University of Oxford (O. H. S., ed. Boase).
Our Memories : Shadows of Old Oxford, privately printed, by C. H. Daniel, 1889-1893.
Wood's Life and Times (O. H. S., ed. A. Clark).
Hearne's Diary (O. H. S., ed. C. E. Doble and D. W. Rannie).

Chapter I

Bodleian MS. 39, f. 38.
Bodleian MS. ab Anthony Wood, 1.
Chronicon Petroburgense (Camden Society), p. 31.

* These deal only with the Gloucester College period.

APPENDIX A

Annales Monastici, Worcester, Rolls Series (ed. Luard), iv., 488, 541.

Historia Monasterii S. Petri Gloucestriæ, Rolls Series (ed. Hart), i. 32.

Calendar of Patent Rolls, Edward I., 1281-1292 (John Giffarde).

Chapter II

Cambridge Documents, i. 379.

Brian Twyne, 22, 166, and following.

Christchurch Letters (Camden Society), p. 56.

Munimenta Academica, 627.

Bodleian Library, Wiltshire Charters, 13.

A deed dated 1371 in the Chapter Library at Canterbury, O, 139.

Literæ Cantuarienses, edited by J. Brigstocke Sheppard, LL.D., vol. i., pp. 358, 392, 414, 415, 417; vol. ii., pp. xxv, 222, 332, 443; vol. iii., p. 14.

History from Marble, by Thomas Dingley (Camden Society), vol. ii., pp. 114, cccxix.

Historical MSS. Commission, Fourteenth Report, App., Part VIII., pp. 123, 124, 179, 182, 183; Fifth Report, p. 451.

Harleian MS. 638, f. 250.

Harleian MS. 308, f. 87b.

Wood MS., F, 33, 103.

H. Anstey, Epistolæ Academicæ.

Chapter III

Newcome's History of the Abbey of St. Albans, 1795, pp. 160, 194, 232, 287, 307, 331, 347, 380, 449, 478.

Gesta Abbatum Monasterii S. Albani, edited by H. T. Riley, iii. 410, 447, 456, 467, 496.

Registrum Abbatiæ Johannis Whethamstede, edited by
   H. T. Riley, i. 452, 458, 462, 473; ii. 382, 390, 416,
   419, 431.
Johannis Amundesham Annales Mon. S. Albani, edited
   by H. T. Riley, i. 34, 40, 154, 161; ii. 200, 256, 264,
   271, 105-112, 292, 307.
Scriptorum Illustrium Majoris Britanniæ, by John Bale,
   p. 592.

Chapter IV

Walsingham's Historia Anglicana, edited by H. T. Riley,
   M.A., ii. 189-192.
Chronicon Abbatiæ Rameseiensis, edited by W. Dunn
   Macray, p. 417.
Epistolæ Academicæ (O. H. S., ed. H. Anstey), 21, 62, 242.
Wood MS., D, 172.
The Obedientiaries Book of the Abbey of Abingdon
   (Camden Society).
Dugdale's Monasticon, iii. 160.
Historia Monasterii S. Petri Gloucestriæ, i. 32-35.
Munimenta Academica, 634.
Letters and Papers, Foreign and Domestic, Henry VIII.,
   1517, vol. ii., App. 33; 1534, 1539, vol. vii., pp. 101,
   129, 684.
Gutch's Collectanea Curiosa, i. 264.
MS. Registrum Curiæ Cancellarii, 1527-1543, Arch. Univ.
   Oxon, E, E, E, f. 194b.
Acts and Monuments, by John Foxe, 1846, vol. v.,
   pp. 421-428, 455.
British Museum Additional MSS. 6769, 274.
Wilkins' Concilia, 2, 594, 717.
Benedictina sive Constitutiones Benedicti XII. ad
   Monachos Nigros, printed by Egidius de Gourmont,
   Paris.

APPENDIX A

Chapter V

Leicester's Commonwealth, 1584, pp. 42, 80.
Foley's Records of the English Province of the Society of Jesus, Ser. 7, 522 ; v., 708.
Letters and Patents, Foreign and Domestic, Henry VIII., 1540-1541, vol. xvi. ; 1488, sec. 30.
Queen Elizabeth and the Catholic Hierarchy (Bridgett and Knox), pp. 76-79.
Brady's Episcopal Succession, ii., 281.
State Papers, Domestic, 1547-1580, p. 566.
State Papers, Domestic, 1591, p. 29.
Wood MS., F, 28, pp. 310 and following.
Rymer's Fœdera, xiv., 754.
Calendar of State Papers, Domestic, 1629 (Richard Corbet).
Plot's Natural History of Oxfordshire, cap. 6, sec. 77.
Report on Historical MSS., Second Report, p. 73.
Oxford Topography (O. H. S.), by H. Hurst, p. 99.
History of St. John's College, by W. H. Hutton, pp. 13, 21.
Register of St. John's College.
MS. Letters of Henry Russell belonging to C. M. Bering Berington, Esq., of Little Malvern.
Dugdale MSS.
Wood's City of Oxford (O. H. S.), vol. iii., pp. 259 and following.

Chapter VI

Calendar of State Papers, Domestic, 1639-1640, p. 358.
Weld's History of the Royal Society.
Calendar of State Papers, Domestic, 1644, p. 27.
The Register of the Parliamentary Visitation (ed. Burrows), Camden Society, p. 236.
Wood's Life and Times (O. H. S.), i. 465, 226 ; iii., 241.

Gulielmi Camdeni et Illustrium Virorum ad G. Camdenum Epistolæ, London, 1691; Letters 252, 254, 255, 261, 262, 265, 266, 270, 272, 273, and 276.

Report on Historical MSS., 6th Report, p. 167.

Gloucester Hall Customs Univ. Archiv. Oxon., D. 27, i., and D. 25, A. (There is a copy of these papers in the library of Worcester College which has been used.)

Aubrey's Brief Lives, vol. i., pp. 26-28, 225, 226; vol. ii., p. 37.

Wallis v. Maidwell, by T. W. Jackson (O. H. S., Collectanea, vol. i., p. 288).

Chapter VII

The Heretic Teacher confuted by His Orthodox Disciple; a Book confirming Traditions and exposing the Sophistries of Benjamin Woodroffe, by Francis Prossalentes, Amsterdam, 1706.*

Second edition of the above, with introduction by A. Moustoxudos, Athens, 1862.*

Historical MSS. Commission, 12th rep., App. VII., pp. 4496; MSS. of S. H. Le Fleming.

Luttrell's Letters, vol. ii., p. 583.

The Sufficiency of the Sacred Writings shown in two Dialogues between George Aptal and George Maroules, Benjamin Woodroffe, their Teacher, presiding, etc., Oxford, 1704.*

Union Review, vol. i., pp. 493, 499, 553; vol. ii., p. 650.

Missionarium, or a Collection of Tracts and Papers lately written against the Missioners or Papal Agents in England, London, 1705, by the Rev. E. Stephens. (This volume is Bodleian, 4to., Rawl., 564. The British Museum copy is defective.)

* These volumes are in Greek. The title has been translated.

APPENDIX A

Historical MSS. Commission, 5th Rep., p. 377. MSS. of J. R. Pine-Coffin.

A Vindication of Christianity from and against the Scandals of Popery in a Letter to a Roman Catholic Gentleman, pp. 22, 23 (1704).

A Model of a College to be settled in the University for the Education of some Youths of the Greek Church, Wood, 276, A. 381.

The Confusion of Popery in England, p. 2.

The Orthodox Church of the East in the Eighteenth Century, by George Williams, 1868.

Dodsley's Old English Plays (ed. Hazlitt), vol. xii., p. 165.

Tanner MSS., 33, 58. Petition of Joseph Giorgoreene, Archbishop of Samos in Greece.

Examinis et Examinantis Examen, etc., by B. Woodroffe, D.D., Oxford, 1700 (Dedication).

Letters of Humphrey Prideaux to John Ellis (Camden Society), pp. 7, 23, 26, 31, 40.

Neale's Holy Eastern Church, ii. 384.

Calendar of Treasury Papers, 1697-1701, vol. lxix., p. 51; 1702-1707, vol. lxxxvii., pp. 113, 142; vol. xcv., p. 11; vol. xcvi., p. 104; vol. xcvii., p. 27; vol. xcix., p. 115.

Hearne's Diary, i., 339; and iv., 350.

Pearson's Levant Chaplains.

Chapter VIII

A Sermon preached June 1, 1699, at Feckenham in Worcestershire, before the Trustees appointed by Sir Thomas Cookes, Bart., to manage his Charity given in that place by John Baron, M.A., and Fellow of Balliol College, in Oxford, 1699.

A Sermon [on 1 Tim. vi. 17-19] preached at Feckenham in Worcestershire, before the Trustees, etc., by Benjamin Woodroffe, Oxford, 1700, 4to.

The Case of Dr. Woodroffe, Madam Marbury, etc., in Chancery, and the Written Paper Madam Marbury left in the Court, 10 July, 1705, 4to., Rawl., 584.

Worcester College MS. Brief for the Plaintiff, Attorney-General *v.* Winford.

Journals of the House of Commons, 1702, vol. xiii., pp. 843, 863.

Journals of the House of Lords, vol. xvii., pp. 27, 86, 89, 92, 93-95 ; vol. xviii., 19, 29, 43, 58, 62, 80, 100.

Memoir of Richard Busby, D.D., by G. F. R. Barker.

History of Balliol College, by H. W. C. Davis.

Lansdowne MSS., 655, ff. 36, 37.

Hearne's Diary (O. H. S.), iv. 383.

The Case of Gloucester Hall, in Oxford, rectifying the False Stating thereof, by Dr. Woodroffe, Canon, attributed to John Baron.

Ballard MSS., 4., 25 ; 21., 138, 142 ; 9., 32, 64 ; 12., 142 ; 21., 53 ; 21., 105 ; 34., 102 ; 21., 41, 42.

Nash's Worcestershire, i. 440 ; ii. 408, 443.

Brit. Mus. Add. MSS. 28,942, p. 287.

Parker's Ephemeris, 1710.

Chapters IX., X. and XI

These chapters are drawn for the most part from the Registers of Worcester College already referred to. The following volumes have also been used :

The Journals of the two Houses of Parliament in Connection with the Bills for dealing with the Eaton Foundations.

APPENDIX B

Printed Copies of the two Bills regulating the Eaton Foundation.
A Printed Copy of the Will of George Clark.
Cox's Recollections of Oxford.
Wordsworth's Social Life at the Universities.
Burgon's Lives of Twelve Good Men.
Robinson's Oxford in the Eighteenth Century.
Dr. King's Anecdotes for His Own Times.

B.—THE NORTHERN CAMERÆ

Mr. T. W. Jackson has kindly furnished us with another theory as to the arrangement of the northern cameræ. It was too late to incorporate it in the volume where this matter was discussed. Starting from the undoubted fact that certain five chambers on the north side were arranged in the following order, going from east to west, Abingdon, Christchurch, Canterbury (afterwards Westminster), Gloucester, Norwich and St. Albans, he suggests that St. Albans was the most westerly camera on the north side; that Gloucester occupied the camera with the courtyard in front of it on the western side of the inner gateway, shown in Loggan's picture; that Westminster was on the east of the same gateway, and Abingdon east of it. Thus he holds that none of the old buildings now standing on the north side are at present identified. The chief arguments in favour of this theory are: 1. That it will fit in with all the known measurements. 2. That it accords more closely with tradition. Though it does not square with Wood, it is more closely in agreement with him than the theory given in Chapter II., and it is in agreement with the very probable tradition that the Gloucester Chamber was that afterwards occupied by the Principal of the Hall. The chief objection to it is that it presupposes that part of the St. Albans camera projecting into the quadrangle was pulled down between 1545 and the date of Loggan's sketch.

He would point out that no theory can be put forward with any feeling of certainty. The theories mentioned have all alike to face the difficulty that the conveyances make no mention of the inner gateway, and it is quite possible that the changes in the sixteenth century were more extensive than is generally imagined.

C.—THE MEMBERS OF GLOUCESTER HALL

A ROUGH list of members of Gloucester Hall, which we have compiled from material afforded by the invaluable Foster's Alumni Oxonienses,* presents some features of interest. The list includes not only those who matriculated from Gloucester Hall, but also those who took their degrees at Gloucester Hall, though their names do not occur in the matriculation register, or, if they do occur, are attributed to some other College or Hall. Between 1570, when the list becomes fairly complete, and 1714, when Worcester College was founded, we have counted 1,050 members of Gloucester Hall, an average of only seven matriculations a year. Of these 350 occur before 1600, 400 between 1600 and 1643, when the effect of the Civil Wars was felt very severely, and the remaining 350 between 1643 and 1714. Thus it will be seen that the annual matriculations during the prosperous period of the Hall averaged from ten to twelve a year. One or two other factors must be taken into consideration. It is almost certain that during the period when the Hall was a

* This work has been used, as the O. H. S. register was not complete, and we have in consequence preferred to use it throughout, even where the results differ from those given by the published portion of the O. H. S. register.

APPENDIX C

refuge for the Roman Catholics, it included a certain proportion of members who, being precluded by religious scruples from matriculating, only remained so long as the University would allow them to dispense with this formality; and the pronounced Catholic reputation of Gloucester Hall would lead one to suppose that the number of such students was large. Secondly, during this early period the Hall probably included a fair number of permanent residents, and we have seen that in 1568 their number was a very large one. Thirdly, an examination of the list leads one to an almost irresistible conclusion that the matriculation system was extremely lax. In no other way can one account for the manner in which the numbers of matriculations fluctuated from year to year. For instance, in 1574 we find 35 matriculations all in January; in the two succeeding years there were none at all, and in 1577 there were 15, in 1578 there were 33, and again in 1579 and 1580 there were none at all. One would therefore argue that the Hall either saved up its students in order that as many as possible might matriculate at one time, or that they did not matriculate at all till the University insisted on it. If any such irregularity as this existed, it was inevitable that some should slip through the net and pass through Gloucester Hall without having matriculated at all. And it is very noticeable how many of those who were undoubtedly at Gloucester Hall are not to be found in the matriculation lists.

In 850 cases the origin of the students at the Hall has been noted. Far the largest proportion, 15 per cent., came from Wales, though I know absolutely no reason for this. All the counties in the West of England were very well represented. Gloucester came second to Wales with 10 per cent.; then followed Devon, 8 per cent.; Middlesex, 8 per cent., and Cornwall 7 per cent.; Somerset, Wilts,

Worcester, Warwickshire, and Oxford, all had between 4 and 5 per cent. No other county was at all liberally represented, but it is noticeable that the representation gets smaller the further east we go, and the percentage for Norfolk and Suffolk is virtually nil. Foreigners number hardly 1 per cent., and in spite of the statement of Wood, Irishmen were only 2 per cent. But that nation always appears to be more numerous than it really is.

Altogether Wales, Gloucester, Devon, Cornwall and Somerset were responsible for no less than 45 per cent. of the members of the Hall.

As to age, there were more deviations from the average at Gloucester Hall than at other Colleges. Quite a number of those who matriculated were well advanced in years; while in the other direction may be quoted the case of the five members of the Fitz James family, who all matriculated in March, 1581, aged respectively seven, nine, ten, eleven, and twelve, or the four Butlers, who matriculated in August, 1593, aged from ten upwards.

The indications as to condition given in the Register of matriculations are extremely uncertain, but one gathers that Gloucester Hall was recruited fairly evenly from all ranks of society, not excluding the highest; perhaps there was a slight predominance of the clergy, but it was not very marked.|

D.—THE PRESENT CONSTITUTION OF THE COLLEGE

THE constitution of the College till the latter half of the present century remained unaltered, save for its enlargement by the incorporation of the Clarke and Eaton Foundations. By the first Universities Commission serious and vital changes were made, which were followed up by the second Commission with others also of an important character. As a result of the first Commission, the original Statutes of the College were superseded by ordinances, contemplating the possibility of statutes based upon them, which were, however, never drawn up. These ordinances were again superseded by the present Statutes, which were the work of the Commission of 1877. The sum of the changes effected at these two stages has been the abolition ᴄ Founder's Kin claims; the extinction of the succession of scholars to Fellowships; the removal of restrictions in the case of Fellowships, save the retention of one Fellow in Holy Orders, while, under the old constitution, there was only one permanently Lay Fellow, the librarian; the reduction of the number of Fellowships from nineteen to nine, or at the most ten; and the consolidation of the Finney Foundation into a single scholarship. Of the Fellows, two at least must be resident within the College walls; four are to be Tutors or Bursars; one may be a Professor-Fellow; the others may be Prize-Fellows, elected on examination. The tenure is for seven years, with re-election, save in the case of the Prize-Fellows, as such.

Of the three officers of the College, two, the Vice-Provost and the Dean, are appointed annually; the third, the Bursar, for a period of three years, or at most of five.

In the case of the scholarships, the original limitations have been retained, always with the provision that the candidate shall satisfy the examiners. Thus, the Eaton Scholarships are for sons of clergymen; the Cookes Scholarships for candidates from Bromsgrove. The Clarke, the Barnes, and the Finney Scholarships are subject to no restrictions.

The Statutes provide for nineteen scholarships; but through the diminution of the College revenue, their number is for the time reduced to twelve, of which only four are open scholarships. On the other hand, the College has for some years past provided a number of small exhibitions, which are awarded upon examination.

The Visitor of the College, who used to be the Bishop of Worcester, the Bishop of Oxford, and the Vice-Chancellor of the University conjointly, is now the Lord High Chancellor on behalf of the Crown.

INDEX

* Signifies that the biography of the member of Worcester College or its predecessors is in the "Dictionary of National Biography."

ABBOT, Archbishop, 133
Abbotesbury, Abbey of, 23, 61
Abingdon, 116
   Abbey of, 23, 26, 29, 34, 63, 87
   Abbot of, 18, 24, 60, 70, 76
   Chapters at, 3, 4, 6, 21
Adams, Rev. E. C., 237
Aegidius, Parish of St., 81
Alcorne, Mrs. Margaret, 201, 212
Aldrich, Dean, 217
Aleppo, 138
Alexandria, 138
*Allen, Thomas, 97, 106, 111, 119, 124, 125
All Souls College, 205
Allyn, John, 99
Amesbury, 6
Amphlett, 168
  ,,   Edward, 223
Amsterdam, 145
Amundesham, John, 50, 51
Anne, Queen, 141, 177
Antioch, 138
Antwerp, 147
Appelton Ridale, 44
Aptal, George, 144, 145
  ,,   John, 145
Aristotle Hall, 81
Armagh, Usher, Archbishop of, 110
Arnold, Thomas, 193, 198
Arran, Earl of, 186
Arundel, Countess of, 98
  ,,   Earl of, 99

Athelney, monastery at, 23
*Atherton, Bishop, 123
Atterbury, Bishop, 186
Aubrey, John, 103, 109, 121
Augustinians, 3

BABINGTON, Dr., 95
Bacheworth, 44
Bacle, John, 81
Bagley Wood, 104
*Bagshaw, Christopher, 102, 119
*Bainbridge, John, 126
Ballard Letters, 162
Balliol College, 1, 104, 120, 163-165
Bancroft, John, 94
Bardney, Abbey of, 23
   Abbot of, 6
*Barksdale, Clement, 111, 127, 218
Barnes, Mr., 210, 237
Baron, John, 156, 163-165
Basle, 73
Baston, Robert, 10
*Bathurst, Ralph, 123, 125
Battle, Abbey of, 23, 24
Baumgarten, Mr., 237
Baxendale, Mr., 194
Beaulieu, 51-53
Beaumont Palace, 10, 11, 153
   Street, 184
Bec, Abbey of, 23
Bell, Rev. G. C., 212

INDEX

Belvoir, Prior of, 53
Benedict XII., 20, 41, 58, 70
Benedictines, 2, 6, 11, 16, 21, 41
    Constitutions of, 21, 42
Besils, Sir Peter, 49
Binney, Bishop, 197, 225
*Bishop, William, 98
Black Boy, The, 184
Blackwell, 65
*Blackwell, George, 97, 98
Bland, Thomas, 93
Blandford St. Mary, 210
Blechynden, Richard, 176, 182, 185, 223, 227
*Bloxam, Andrew, 197
    ,,   Dr., 219
Bodley, Thomas, 126
Bologna, 18, 19
Boniface, 22
Boniface VIII., 74
Bonner, Bishop, 86
Botley Bridge, 92
Bourchier, Roger, 181, 205
*Bourne, Robert, 197
Bramsford, 209
Brasenose College, 205
Brickenden, F. H., 190
Bridges, Grey, 106
Bridges, John, 93
Briggs, Henry, 110
Brimsfield, 4, 5
Broadgates Hall, 105, 110
Brok, William de, 68, 76
Bromsgrove, 158, 169
Brookes, Henry, 187
*Brounfelde, Edmund, 87
Browne, Jonathan, 110
Buckingham College, Cambridge, 25
*Budden, John, 124
Bullock, Miss, 217
    ,,   Mr., 223
Burgon, Dean, 193, 197, 199
Burnell's Inn, 26
Burton, Prior of, 23, 61
    ,,   R., 107
    ,,   William, 110
Bury St. Edmunds, Abbey of, 23, 34, 38, 63, 85, 87
Busby, Richard, 159
Bushop, Anthony, 97
Butler, family of, 34
Bybery Church, 66
Bynham, Prior of, 53

CAJETAN, 98
Callinicus, Patriarch, 138

Calton, Thomas de, 68
Cambridge, 22, 25
Camden, William, 106, 224
Canterbury, Archbishop of, 17, 23, 42, 49, 79, 120, 158, 168
    Christchurch, 23, 28, 49
    College, 23
    Province of, 2, 3, 20
    St. Augustine's, 23, 32, 61
Cantlett, Anthony, alias Stanton, 102
Cardoinus, Camillus, 124
*Carew, John, 121, 122
Carmelites, 3, 10, 11, 38, 90
*Carr, Robert James, 196
Carter, E. S., 236
Cartwright, William, 116
Catesby, Lady, 97, 98
*   ,,   Robert, 121, 122
    ,,   Sir William, 98
Catholics at Gloucester Hall, 97-103
Chalcedon, Bishop of, 98
Chambers, John, 93
Chandos, Lord, 106
Charlett, Dr., 163
Charterhouse School, 202
Cheltenham, John, 31
Cheltyham, Richard, 31
Chertsey, Abbey of, 23
    Abbot of, 6
Cheshire, salt mines in, 141
Chester, monastery at, 23, 61
Chettle, Thomas, 209
    ,,   William, 168, 209
Chichele, 24
Chillington, 4
Chipping Norton, 66
Christchurch, Canterbury, 23, 28, 49
    Oxford, 82, 91, 202, 205
Clare, Gilbert, 9
Clarke, Dr. George, 185, 189, 204, 218, 222, 224
*Clayton, Thomas, 110, 124
Clement, 21
Clement VIII., 98
Cluett, Richard, 110
Clyve, Richard de, 76
Cock and Bottle, The, 184
Colchester, Priory of, 23, 25
*Cole, William, 126
Coles, Mrs. Anne, 97
Collins, J., 222
*Collis, John Day, 198, 217
Colpoys, 235
Combermere, Viscount, 194
Compounder, the last Grand, 194
Compton, Walter, 30

INDEX 263

Constantine, Stephen, 145, 147, 150
Cooke, Edward, 211
" Samuel, 212
Cookes, David, 168
" John, 222
" Sir Thomas, 85, 154-168, 224
Corbet, Richard, 94
Corcyra, 139, 146
Cornwall Close, 10
Corpus Christi College, Oxford, 85
Corro, Anthony de, 124
*Coryate, Thomas, 121, 122, 226
Cotswolds, King of the, 106
*Cotton, Dr. R. L., 190, 193, 210, 212, 224, 225
Courtenay, William de, 17, 42, 79
Cove, Stephen de, 8
Coventry, monastery of, 23, 24, 61
*Coxe, H. O., 46, 199, 226
* " Richard, 126
Craven, W. D., 236
Crewe, Nathaniel Lord, 211
Critopoulos Metrophanes, 133
Croke, Richard, 82
Cromwell, Thomas, 82
Croyland, Abbey of, 25
Cuddesdon Palace, 94
Cumnor, 95

DAMEROS, Paul, 145
Damiral, Michael, 145
Daniel, Rev. C. H., 237
Daventry, Abbey of, 23
Davies, John, 126
" Sir John, 126
Dawson, Thomas, 116
Dee, John, 126
Delabere, Anthony, 84
" John, 103, 120
Denchworth, 193
Dent, Rev. Benjamin, 211
Dickenson Estate, 141
*Digby, Kenelm, 121, 122, 125
Dinedor, 210
Dingley, John, alias Falkner, 101
" Sir Edward, 187
Doddington, William, 91, 92
Dominicans, 3
Dorchester, Secretary, 94
Douai, 98, 99
Drusius, John, 124
Dudley, Robert, Earl of Leicester, 95, 102
Dunwych, John, 81
Dupper, Mr. Edward, 211

Durham College, 22
County of, 203

EATON, Dr. Byrom, 117, 121, 128, 207, 223
" Mrs. Sarah, 120, 189, 207
Ecclesdale, Lancs, 140, 141
Eden, 85
Edmundsbury, see Bury St. Edmunds
Edward II., 10
Eleanor, Queen, 6
Elizabeth, Queen, 91
Ellis, John, 129
" John, Yeoman of the Guard, 89
Ellismere, William, 81
Ely, Abbey of, 25
"Ephemeris," Parker's, 172
Essex, Earl of, 126
Evesham, Abbey of, 23, 26, 61, 85
Abbot of, 6, 24
Evesham, Philip, Abbot of, 85
Exeter College, 105
Eynsham, Abbey of, 23, 49, 88
Abbot of, 86

FALKLAND, Lord, 115
Falkner, John, alias Dingley, 101
Feckenham, 158, 164, 166
*Feckenham, John, 85, 169
Fell, Samuel, 110
Feteplace, John, 97
Finney, James, 203
Fish, J. H., 236
Flanders, Governor of, 147
Florence, Envoy of, 149
Fonthill, 4
*Foote, Samuel, 168, 182, 186, 226
Fowler, John, alias Francis Geoffry, 102
Franciscans, 3
Frasthorp, John, 81
Frouceter, Walter, 66
Fulwell, 207

GABRIEL, R. Burd, 208, 212, 220
Galys, John, 31
Garbrand, Herks, 115
" Tobias, 109, 115, 119
Gardiner, Daniel, 106
*Garnier, Thomas, Dean of Winchester, 196, 232
" " Dean of Lincoln, 196, 232
Garret, 84

INDEX

Gatagre, Richard, 97, 119
*Geddes, Michael, 121
Gent, William, 126
Geoffrey, Francis, alias Fowler, 102
Georgirenes, Joseph, 135
Giffarde, Elias, 4
  ,,   John, 4-9, 11, 13, 69
  ,,   Osbert, 4
  ,,   Walter, 4
Gilbert, William, 110
Giles, John, 208
Glastonbury, Abbey of, 23, 34
  A monk of, 81
Glin, John, 89
Gloucester, Abbey of St. Peter's, 2, 4, 5, 20-24, 34, 69
  Abbot of, 7, 28, 29
  Bishop of, 86, 169
  Gilbert Clare, Earl of, 9
  Humphrey, Duke of, 9, 10, 46
  Robert Haymon, Earl of, 9
Gloucester College, 1-88
  Arms in, 34
  Cameræ in, 26-34
  Chapel of, 35, 48, 49, 55, 56
  Constitutions of, 22, 23
  Dissolution of, 89-92
  Enlargement of, 20
  Foundation of, 3
  Heresy at, 84
  Kitchen of, 36
  Library of, 35, 45-48
  Members of, 86-88
  Refectory of, 35
  Site of, 9-11
  Vestiarium of, 35
Gloucester Hall, 92-181
  Catholics at, 97-101
  Chapel of, 108
  Customs of, 112, 113
  Decay of, 118
  Foundation of, 92-96
  Greeks at, 128-153
  Lawsuit as to, 93, 94
  Library of, 111
  Members of, 121-127
  Repair of, 131
  Strangers at, 96, 97
  Survey of, 177
*Godolphin, John, 123
Godwyne, Daniel, 212
Goldie, Rev. F., 33
Goldwell, Thomas, 100
Gondomar, 134
Good, Dr., 120
Goodenough, Dr., 192

Gower, Dr. William, 182, 186, 188, 209, 218, 223, 327
Greek College at Gloucester Hall, 2
Gregory IX., Pope, 74
*Grenville, John, Earl of Bath, 127
*Greswell, Richard, 197, 199, 220, 221, 225
  ,,   William Parr, 197
Grey, Lord, of Ruthin, 51
Griffin, Roger, 110
*Griffith, Matthew, 126
Griffiths, E. G. C., 236
Gunter, Richard, 88
Gwynne, Dr., 126

*HAAK, Theodore, 125
Hagenport, John de, 8
Hague, 147
Hales, Alexander, 218
  ,,   John, 110
Halle, Greek College at, 151
Hannay, James, 192, 212, 225
Harbin, Mr., 202
Harcourt, Philip, 222
*Harding, Bishop, 197, 225
*Harrison, Sedgwick, 126
Hart Hall, 202
Hartlebury School, 169, 178, 190
Hatfield Peverelle, Prior of, 53
Hatton, Chancellor, 93
Hawley, John, 103, 106, 107
Hawvill, William de, 8
Haymon, Robert, 9
Haynes, John, 82
Hearne, 10, 146, 202, 204
Helm, Henry de, 7
Henry III., 5
Hereford, Bishop of, 87
  ,,   Marquis of, 115
  ,,   Prior of, 53
Heyworth, William, 42, 44
Hickes, George, 166
Hierapolis, 138
Hill Marton, 206
Hippolytus, Dr., 146
Hoggeston, 210
Holden, W. R., 217
Hole, Mr., 223
Holford, Lady Elizabeth, 202, 224
  ,,   Sir William, 202
Holland, Mrs. Susanna, 97
Holsoye, Stephen, 81
Holywell Mill, 116
Homer, George, 145
  ,,   Simon, 145, 148
Honsom, Lawrence, 68, 76

INDEX

Hooke, A., 236
Hospitallers, 8, 9
Hudson, Dr., 176
*Hugo, Thomas, 198
Humphrey, Duke of Gloucester, 9, 10, 46
Hyde, Abbey of, 23, 34, 37, 61
Hythe Bridge, 183

INGE, Dr. William, 195
Ingram, Mrs. Joan, 97
,, Richard, 97
Irishry at Gloucester Hall, 103
Ixworth, Robert, 72

JACOBSTOW, 105
James, John, 89
Jerusalem, 138
Johnson, Dr., 186
Jones, Chancellor, 211
,, Charles Wake, 222
Juries, grand, of Worcestershire, 165, 167

KADEGRAFT, 30
Kay, Mr., 209
*Kedermyster, Richard, 88
Keate, Sir H. O., 222
*Kelly, Edward, alias Talbot, 124
Kertlington, 104
Kettle Hall, 116
Kidderminster, 169, 178
King, Dr., 186
,, Robert, Bishop of Oxford, 91, 93
King's Head, The, 184
Kingsley Club, 244
*Kingsley, Henry, 198, 237
*Kirton, Edmund, 48, 72, 73, 87
*Kitchin, Anthony, 84, 86, 87

LAMBETH PALACE, 156
Lancaster, William, 175
Landon, Dr. Whittington, 183, 190, 194, 225, 227
*Langdon, John, 88
Laud, Archbishop, 113
*Lawerne, John, 88
Laws, John, 81
Lawson, Henry, 99
Laycock, Mrs., 211
Ledbury, Thomas, 36, 50
Leghorn, 149, 150
Leicester, Robert Dudley, Earl of, 95, 102

Levant Company, 136, 139, 147, 151
Lewis, Elizabeth, 202
Lichfield, 168
Lincoln, Bishop of, 8, 51
Littybury, 34
Llandaff, Kitchin, Bishop of, 87
,, Brounfeld, Bishop of, 87
,, Salley, Bishop of, 87
Loder, John, 211
Loggan, 29, 37, 45, 131
Lombard, Peter, 75
Longespee, Maud, 5, 8
Longsport, 29
Loteris, Eve, 8
Louvain, 100, 147
*Lovelace, Richard, 121, 226
Lowndes, Mr., 140
,, Robert, 222
Lucar, Cyril, 133
Ludlow, 103
Lyford, 208

MAGDALENE COLLEGE, Cambridge, 25
Magdalen Hall, 172, 176
Malan, E. C., 236
Malmesbury, Abbot of, 11, 12, 28
Abbey of, 13, 20, 23, 28, 29, 33, 37, 43, 54, 61
Manders, Dr., 172
Manston, John, 81
Maplett, John, 115
Marbury, William and Richard, 174
March, Baldon, 94
Marchal, Roger, 81
Mare, Thomas de la, 21, 41, 59, 68
Margaret, Queen, 10
Maroules, George, 144
Martin V., Pope, 49, 52
Mary, Virgin, 11
Mason, Mr., 164
*Meara, Dermitius, 125
Mechlin, 147
Men, Horman, 82
Meredith, William, 99
Merritt, Christopher, 111, 125
Merton College, 1, 46
Meules, Nicholas de, 10
Michelney, Abbey of, 23, 61
Middelburg, 147
Middleton, Abbey of, 23
Miller, Rev. John, 194, 198, 226
,, Thomas, 97
Moore, John, 192
Moote, John de la, 41, 43
Morgan, Hugh, 189

INDEX

Moulden, Mary, 120
Moustoxudos, A., 146
Muckleston, Rev. Rowland, 210, 221
Mylys, 81
*Mylling, Thomas, 87

*Nash, Treadway Russell, 198, 224, 225
Neen Solars, 210
New College, 203
Newdigate Prize, 197
Newfoundland, 96
*Newman, Francis William, 199
Newton, Sir Charles T., 199
Nixon, W., 236
Northampton, 21, 48
Norton, Thomas, 81
Norwich, Priory of, 23, 25, 28, 32, 37, 43, 60
Nuneham Courtenay, 118, 176

Olevian, Francis, 124
Ormonde, Duke of, 163, 166
Osney, Abbot of, 65
    Bishop of, 90
Oxford. See under Colleges
    Bishop of, 2, 91, 93, 168
    Mayor of, 38, 88

Pakenham, 65
Palmer, William, 96
    ,, William, 197
Palmes, William, 141
Paris, 18, 41
    Greek College at, 151
Parsons the Jesuit, 102
Pate, Bishop Richard, 100
*Peckham, Sir George, 96, 98
Pembroke College, 110, 202
*Percy, George, 127
Pershore, 30
    Abbey of, 23, 34
    Abbot of, 30, 86
Peterborough, Abbey of, 23, 24
Piddington, 207
Pine, R. E., 225
Pinyngses, Henry, 100
Plato's Well, 38, 39
Pocock, Dr., 129
*Poole, Bishop A. W., 197
Portuguese Ambassador, 147, 149
Powell, Edmund, 89
Preston, 225
*Price, Bonamy, 198, 199

Prideaux, Humphrey, 129
Prossalentes, Francis, 143, 150
Purton Estate, 206
Pusey, Dr., 194
    ,, Philip, 217
Pym, Alexander, 105
    ,, John, 105, 110
    ,, William, 222

Rainolds, Edmund, 98, 110
Ramsey, Abbey of, 23, 25, 31, 34
Read, 33
Reading, 21
    Abbot of, 23, 76
Rewley, Abbey of, 9, 10, 38
Ringstede, Richard, 72
Rivers, Earl, 174
Robinson, Richard, 231
Robsart, Amy, 95
Rochester, Bishop of, 88, 120
    Abbey of, 23, 24, 60
*Rogers, J. E. Thorold, 198, 225
Rome, English College at, 100, 102
Romsey, Richard, 34
Ross, John, 10
Rowham, Edward, 65
Rowing, 232-236
Royal Society, 125
Rump Hall, 137
Rumsey, William, 123
Russell, Henry, 102
    ,, John, 30

St. Albans, Abbey of, 16, 28, 34, 37, 40-56
    Abbots of, 41.45, 79
St. Alban Hall, 84
St. Aldate's, 26
St. Benet's of Hulme, 25
St. Bernard's College, Oxford, 93
St. Edmund's Hall, 23, 172
St. John's College, 2, 35, 95, 103, 113, 153, 171, 176, 183
St. John the Baptist's Hall, 2, 7, 93; and see Gloucester Hall
St. John of Jerusalem, Hospitallers of 8, 9
St. Mary's Church, Oxford, 73, 82, 95
St. Mary's College, Oxford, 92
St. Mary Hall, Oxford, 176
St. Neot's, Priory of, 23
St. Nicholas, Parish of, Oxford, 90
St. Peter's in the East, Oxford, 23
St. Thomas, Church of, Oxford, 97, 99
Salisbury, 6, 21, 40
    Earl of, 5

INDEX

Salley, Miles, 87
Salusbury, John, 85
Sambatch, John, 111
Samos, Archbishop of, 135
Sandys, Waterworks, 110
Sapphira, 146
Sawyer, Widow, 102
Scholefield, J. C., 237
Scudamore, Viscount, 222
Sheffield, Dr. William, 182, 189, 225
Sheldon, Ralph, 99
Sherborne, Monastery of, 23, 85
Shrewsbury, Priory of, 23
Smith, Thomas, 184
Smyrna, 139
Sovereigns, The Allied, 191
Staffordshire, Moorlands of, 203
Stanton, Henry, alias Cantlett, 102
Stanywell, John, 86
Star Chamber, 102
Stephens, Edward, 134, 149, 152
Stocke, William, 95, 96, 102, 119
Stockwell, Nicholas de, 38
    Street, 8, 10, 11, 36, 38, 90
Stoke, Priory of, 23
Stonehouse, George, 130
    ,, Sir Blewet, 130
Stratford, Dr., 175
Strivelin, Battle of, 11
Stubbs, Justinian, 101, 102
*   ,, Philip, 101
Swayton, 120
Sykes, E., 226

TADMARTON, 210
Tardebigg, 168
Tavistock, Abbot of, 23
Taylorian Galleries, 184
Tewkesbury, Abbey of, 23, 33, 86
Thame, 92
Theological Schools, Oxford, 72, 73
Tidswell, R. T., 212
Tower of London, 100
Turkey Company, 137
Twyford, 4
Twyne, Brian, 9, 85
Tynemouth, Prior of, 53
Tyrwhitt, Rev. R. A. J., 226
  ,, T., 246
Tythers, Anthony, 93

UNDERHILL, John, 93
University Commission, 258
University Hall, 1

VENICE, 101

WADHAM COLLEGE, 100, 103
Wadham, Dorothy, 103
  ,, Nicholas, 100, 103
Wainfleete, William of, 172
*Wakeman, John, 86
Walcup, Madame, 130
Walden, Priory of, 25
Waldron, Edward, 190
Wallingford, Richard of, 74
Walkeringham, 207
Walsingham, 98
Walsingham, Thomas, 88
Walyngford, Prior of, 53
Wanley, Samuel, 225
Warner, John, 120
Warren, Thomas, 97
Watson, Idonea, 8
  ,, John, 8
Wellington, Duke of, 194
Westminster Abbey, 23, 28, 61, 86
    Abbot of, 76, 79, 87
Weston-under-Edge, 4
Wheare, Charles, 114
*   ,, Degory, the elder, 105, 107, 114, 119, 224
  ,, Degory, the younger, 114
  ,, John, 111, 114
  ,, Samuel, 114
  ,, William, 114
Whethamstede, John, 22, 27, 36, 42.56
Whetle, William, 81
Whitby, Abbey of, 23
White, Sir Thomas, 92, 93, 95
Whitfield, 186
Whorwood of Holton, 111
Wilberforce, Bishop, 193, 214
Williams, 191
  ,, Sir John, 92
  ,, Walter, 212
Willmot, 154
Winchcombe, Abbey of, 3, 23, 30, 31, 33, 88
    Abbot of, 6, 31
Winchester, St. Mary's, 23
Windauer, Justice, 93
Windsor, Lord, 101
Winford, 210
  ,, Henry, 168
  ,, Sir Thomas, 171
Winslow, 44
Wisbech Castle, 86, 103
Wodehull, H. de, 78
Wodestok, J., 81

INDEX

Wolsey, Cardinal, 82
Wood, Anthony, 9, 10, 34, 87
*Woodroffe, Benjamin, 107, 127-176, 223
Woodroffe's Folly, 153, 174
Woodville, Elizabeth, 87
Woolvercott, 114
Worcester, Bishop of, 100, 158, 167, 168
  County of, 100
  House, 39, 183
  Prior of, 6
  Priory of, 23, 24, 33, 65
  School, 169, 178, 186
Worcester College, Chapel of, 213-217
  Foundation of, 154-182
  Gardens of, 220, 221
  Hall of, 219, 220
  Library of, 217-219
  Pictures of, 223-226
  Plate of, 222, 223
Wrench, Mr. Thomas, 221

Wright, Mr. Blaney, 223
Wyatt, Richard, 116
Wymundham, Prior of, 53
Wyntersulle, William, 44
Wyofton, 24

XANTHEUS, Jeremiah, 152

YEOMEN OF THE GUARD, 89
York, Abbey of St. Mary's, 22, 25
  County of, exhibition for natives of, 210
  Province of, 20
Ysa, John, 44

ZACYNTHUS, 146
Zittau, 152

BILLING AND SONS, PRINTERS, GUILDFORD

AT ALL LIBRARIES AND BOOKSELLERS'.

Universities of Oxford and Cambridge

TWO SERIES OF POPULAR HISTORIES OF THE COLLEGES

To be completed in Twenty-one and Eighteen Volumes respectively.

EACH volume will be written by some one officially connected with the College of which it treats, or at least by some member of that College who is specially qualified for the task. It will contain: (1) A History of the College from its Foundation; (2) An Account and History of its Buildings; (3) Notices of the Connection of the College with any Important Social or Religious Events; (4) A List of the Chief Benefactions made to the College; (5) Some Particulars of the Contents of the College Library; (6) An Account of the College Plate, Windows, and other Accessories; (7) A Chapter upon the best known, and other notable but less well-known Members of the College.

Each volume will be produced in crown octavo, in a good clear type, and will contain about 250 pages (except two or three volumes, which will be thicker). The illustrations will consist of full-page plates, containing reproductions of old views of the Colleges and modern views of the buildings, grounds, etc.

No particular order will be observed in the publication of the volumes. The writers' names are given overleaf.

Price 5s. net per volume.

Catalogue with press notices on application.

These volumes can be ordered through any bookseller, or they will be sent by the Publishers on receipt of the published price and postage.

F. E. ROBINSON & Co.,

20, GREAT RUSSELL STREET, BLOOMSBURY, LONDON.

OXFORD SERIES.

COLLEGES.	
University.	W. CARR, M.A., *Stanhope Essay*, 1884; *Lothian Essay*, 1888; *Arnold Essay*, 1890.
Balliol	H. W. CARLESS DAVIS, M.A., *Fellow of All Souls.*
Merton	B. W. HENDERSON, M.A., *Fellow of Merton; Arnold Essay* 1895.
Exeter	W. K. STRIDE, M.A., *English Essay*, 1896.
Oriel	D. W. RANNIE, M.A., *Stanhope Essay*, 1890; *English Essay*, 1895.
Queen's	Rev. J. R. MAGRATH, D.D., *Provost of Queen's; Stanhope Essay*, 1860; *Johnson Theological Scholar*, 1861.
New	Rev. HASTINGS RASHDALL, M.A., *Tutor of New College; Stanhope Prize*, 1879; *English Essay*, 1883; *Late Fellow of Hertford;* and R. S. RAIT, B.A., *Fellow of New College.*
Lincoln	Rev. ANDREW CLARK, M.A., *Hon. LL.D., St. Andrews; Rector of Great Leighs, Chelmsford; Late Fellow of Lincoln.*
All Souls	C. GRANT ROBERTSON, M.A., *Fellow of All Souls; Stanhope Essay*, 1891.
Magdalen	Rev. H. A. WILSON, M.A., *Fellow and Librarian of Magdalen; Curator of the Bodleian Library.*
Brasenose	J. BUCHAN, B.A., *Exhibitioner of Brasenose; Stanhope Essay*, 1897; *Newdigate Prize*, 1898.
Corpus Christi	Rev. T. FOWLER, D.D., *President of Corpus; Denyer Theological Essay*, 1858; *Professor of Logic*, 1873-1889; *Member of the Visitorial Board; Delegate of the Press, and of the Common University Fund; Late Fellow of Lincoln; Hon. LL.D., Edinburgh; F.S.A.*
Christ Church	Rev. H. L. THOMPSON, M.A., *Late Student and Censor of Christ Church; Vicar of St. Mary's, Oxford; Late Warden of Radley.*
Trinity	Rev. H. E. D. BLAKISTON, M.A., *Fellow and Tutor of Trinity.*
St. John's	Rev. W. H. HUTTON, B.D., *Fellow and Tutor of St. John's; Stanhope Essay*, 1881; *Curator of the Schools; Examining Chaplain to the Bishop of Ely.*
Jesus	E. G. HARDY, M.A., *Fellow and Vice-Principal of Jesus College.*
Wadham	J. WELLS, M.A., *Fellow and Tutor of Wadham; Delegate of Local Examinations for Extension of University Teaching, and for training of Teachers.*
Pembroke	Rev. DOUGLAS MACLEANE, M.A., *Late Fellow of Pembroke.*
Worcester	Rev. C. H. O. DANIEL, M.A., *Fellow and Bursar of Worcester; Fellow of King's College, London,* and W. R. BARKER, B.A., *Late Scholar of Worcester.*
Hertford	S. G. HAMILTON, M.A., *Fellow and Bursar of Hertford; Latin Verse*, 1875; *Hereford Scholar*, 1875; *Gaisford Prize (Verse)*, 1877.
Keble	D. J. MEDLEY, M.A., *Professor of History in Glasgow University; late Tutor of Keble.*

CAMBRIDGE SERIES.

College	Editor
Peterhouse	Rev. T. A. WALKER, LL.D., *Tutor and Dean of Peterhouse; Lightfoot Scholar*, 1884 ; *Whewell Scholar*, 1884.
Clare	J. R. WARDALE, M.A., *Tutor of Clare; Bell Scholar*, 1879 ; *Battie Scholar*, 1881 ; *Late Professor of Latin in University College, Cardiff*.
Pembroke	W. S. HADLEY, M.A., *Fellow and Assistant Tutor of Pembroke*.
Caius	J. VENN, Sc.D., F.R.S., *Fellow of Gonville and Caius*.
Trinity Hall	H. T. TREVOR JONES, M.A., *Late Scholar of Trinity Hall*.
Corpus Christi	Rev. H. P. STOKES, LL.D., *Late Scholar of C.C.C.; Vicar of St. Paul's, Cambridge; Harness Prizeman*, 1877.
King's	Rev. A. AUSTEN LEIGH, M.A., *Provost of King's*.
Queens'	Rev. J. H. GRAY, M.A., *Fellow and Dean of Queens'*.
St. Catharine's	THE LORD BISHOP OF BRISTOL, *Hon. Fellow of St. Catharine's; Late Disney Professor of Archæology*.
Jesus	A. GRAY, M.A., *Fellow and Tutor of Jesus College*.
Christ's	J. PEILE, Litt.D., *Master of Christ's; Formerly Reader in Comparative Philology; Hon. Litt.D., of Dublin*.
St. John's	J. BASS MULLINGER, M.A., *University Lecturer in History; History Lecturer and Librarian of St. John's*.
Magdalene	Rev. G. PRESTON, M.A., *Rector of Great Fransham, Norfolk; Late Fellow of Magdalene*.
Trinity	Rev. A. H. F. BOUGHEY, M.A., *Fellow and Late Tutor of Trinity*; and J. WILLIS CLARK, M.A., *Late Fellow of Trinity; Registrary of the University*.
Emmanuel	E. S. SHUCKBURGH, M.A., *Librarian and Formerly Fellow of Emmanuel*.
Sidney	G. M. EDWARDS, M.A., *Fellow and Tutor of Sidney; Bell Scholar*, 1877, *Davies Scholar*, 1879; *Chancellor's Medallist*, 1880.
Downing	REV. H. W. PETTIT STEVENS, M.A., LL.M., *Vicar of Tadlow; Late Scholar of Downing*.
Selwyn	Rev. A. L. BROWN, M.A., *Tutor and Librarian of Selwyn*.

Some Press Opinions of the Series.

Times.—"We are glad to welcome the first two volumes of what promises to be an excellent series of College Histories. . . . Well printed, handy and convenient in form, and bound in the dark or light blue of either University, these small volumes have everything external in their favour. As to their matter, all are to be entrusted to competent men, who, if they follow in the steps of the first two writers, will produce records full of interest to everybody who cares for our old Universities."

Literature.—"Mr. Robinson has secured an exceptionally good list of contributors, comprising many of the most distinguished men in the academic life of both Universities."

Cape Times.—"A series of Histories of Oxford and Cambridge Colleges by competent writers may be expected to furnish useful aid to the historical student in addition to its claim on the attention of the large class of English-speaking people connected in one way or another with the ancient English Universities. A man's affection for his college is only second to his affection for his home . . . the story of a college aptly told cannot fail to interest a large number of readers, and the publishers who have undertaken to present such stories in full tale deserve well of the people."

Cambridge Review.—"The plan announced by Mr. F. E. Robinson of a series of popular histories of the colleges of Oxford and Cambridge should meet with very general support. Probably far more men are interested in the history of their own college than in that of the University in general."

Court Journal.—"To chronicle the history of the colleges of Oxford and Cambridge is not an undertaking for one man nor even for a pair, each representing his *alma mater*. Mr. F. E. Robinson has done the wisest thing in arranging for the history of every single college to be written by some one of its members specially qualified."

Church Bells.—"We strongly recommend our readers to commence the series at once, and to secure each volume as it appears."

Church Times.—"The excellent series of College Histories."

Daily News.—"Mr. F. E. Robinson's series of College Histories will interest not only the past and present members of the institutions dealt with, but all who possess a taste for that which is quaint and amusing in the manners and customs of our forefathers."

Manchester Courier.—"The series of College Histories projected by Mr. Robinson will be welcome to all 'Varsity men, past, present or future, and their attractive appearance, combined with the modest price at which they are issued, will insure their popularity, independently of the value of the contents."

Literary World.—"The two series have begun well, and the mechanical execution of the volumes is excellent."

Sheffield Daily Telegraph.—"Mr. Robinson is to be congratulated upon the progress of his double series."

Manchester Guardian.—"The idea of a complete series of histories of the colleges in the two Universities is excellent, and one only wonders that it has not been taken up before. . . . They are printed in a fine clear type, and adorned with numerous photographs of the college buildings, reduced facsimiles of Loggan's famous seventeenth-century views serving as frontispieces. Their external appearance is also tasteful."

Guardian.—"For the sake of learning, for the sake of the propagation of that *esprit de corps* which is so valuable to the nation at large, for the sake of auld lang syne, we heartily wish well to College Histories. . . . Mr. F. E. Robinson shows originality and enterprise in projecting a series of histories which shall include every college in Oxford and Cambridge, and he appears to have been fortunate in the writers whose assistance he has procured."